ENTOMOLOGY AND PALYNOLOGY

EVIDENCE FROM THE
NATURAL WORLD

FORENSICS: THE SCIENCE OF CRIME-SOLVING

TITLE LIST

ENTOMOLOGY AND PALYNOLOGY

EVIDENCE FROM THE
NATURAL WORLD

by Maryalice Walker

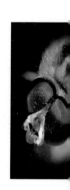

Mason Crest Publishers
Philadelphia

Mason Crest Publishers Inc.
370 Reed Road
Broomall, Pennsylvania 19008
(866) MCP-BOOK (toll free)

First printing
1 2 3 4 5 6 7 8 9 10

Library of Congress Cataloging-in-Publication Data

Walker, Maryalice.
  Entomology and palynology : evidence from the natural world
/ by Maryalice Walker.
      p. cm. — (Forensics, the science of crime-solving)
  Includes index.
  ISBN 1-4222-0032-9   ISBN 1-4222-0025-6 (series)
    1. Criminals—Identification. 2. Criminal investigation. 3.
Forensic sciences. 4. Forensic entomology. 5. Palynology. I.
Title. II. Series.
  HV8073.W33 2006
  363.25—dc22
                                        2005018934

Produced by Harding House Publishing Service, Inc.
www.hardinghousepages.com
Interior and cover design by MK Bassett-Harvey.
Printed in India.

Contents

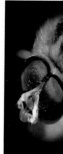

Introduction

By Jay A. Siegel, Ph.D.
Director, Forensic and Investigative Sciences Program
Indiana University, Purdue University, Indianapolis

It seems like every day the news brings forth another story about crime in the United States. Although the crime rate has been slowly decreasing over the past few years (due perhaps in part to the aging of the population), crime continues to be a very serious problem. Increasingly, the stories we read that involve crimes also mention the role that forensic science plays in solving serious crimes. Sensational crimes such as the O. J. Simpson case, or more recently, the Laci Peterson tragedy, provide real examples of the power of forensic science. In recent years there has been an explosion of books, movies, and TV shows devoted to forensic science and crime investigation. The wondrously successful *CSI* TV shows have spawned a major increase in awareness of and interest in forensic science as a tool for solving crimes. *CSI* even has its own syndrome: the *"CSI* Effect,"* wherein jurors in real cases expect to hear testimony about science such as fingerprints, DNA, and blood spatter because they saw it on TV.

The unprecedented rise in the public's interest in forensic science has fueled demands by students and parents for more educational programs that teach the applications of science to crime. This started in colleges and universities but has filtered down to high schools and middle schools. Even elementary school students now learn how science is used in the criminal justice system. Most educators agree that this developing interest in forensic science is a good thing. It has provided an excellent opportunity to teach students science—and they have fun learning it! Forensic science is an ideal vehicle for teaching science for several reasons. It is truly multidisciplinary;

practically every field of science has forensic applications. Successful forensic scientists must be good problem solvers and critical thinkers. These are critical skills that all students need to develop.

In all of this rush to implement forensic science courses in secondary schools throughout North America, the development of grade-appropriate resources that help guide students and teachers is seriously lacking. There are very few college and high school textbooks and none that are appropriate for younger students. That is why this new series: FORENSICS: THE SCIENCE OF CRIME-SOLVING is so important and so timely. Each book in the series contains a concise, age-appropriate discussion of one or more areas of forensic science.

Students are never too young to begin to learn the principles and applications of science. Forensic science provides an interesting and informative way to introduce scientific concepts in a way that grabs and holds the students' attention. FORENSICS: THE SCIENCE OF CRIME-SOLVING promises to be an important resource in teaching forensic science to students twelve to eighteen years old.

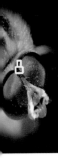

CHAPTER ONE

The Grasshopper's Tale

Several suspects arrived at the police station for questioning about the woman's murder. When Texas police searched one particular suspect, they discovered the grasshopper's missing hind leg in the cuff of the suspect's pant leg. This tiny fragment of an insect placed the suspect with the victim at the time of her death and later helped convict him of murder.

A tiny grasshopper brought the criminal in this case to justice, thanks to the field of *forensics*. Forensics describes any science applied to the law, and includes many categories such as forensic psychology, medicine, and anthropology. Forensic sciences are powerful crime-solving tools because they provide objective evidence—the cold, hard facts—useful in legal cases. The type of forensic science used to solve the grasshopper case is called *forensic entomology*.

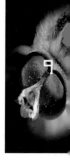

WHAT IS FORENSIC ENTOMOLOGY?

Forensic entomology is the application of the science of insect biology, ecology, and behavior—entomology—to legal cases.

Forensic entomology consists of three fields: medico-legal, urban, and stored-products entomology.

Medico-legal entomology involves using insects to solve violent crimes and to investigate sudden, suspicious, and accidental deaths such as vehicle accidents. Of the three fields, medico-legal entomology receives the most coverage in scientific articles and draws the most fascination among the general public, as well as the most attention on television crime dramas like *C.S.I.* and *Law & Order*. In fact, some scientists use "forensic entomology" to refer to medico-legal entomology alone.

Even the tiniest of evidence—like the leg of a grasshopper—can link a suspect to a crime.

But while medico-legal entomology may seem the most "exciting," urban and stored-products entomology are also important to crime investigation. Urban entomology involves insects in buildings, human-made structures, and other locations in the human environment. Cases in this field usually aim to discover the source of an insect infestation. Stored-products entomology deals with insect infestations in stored food, and aims to determine when and from where insects invaded the food. This field often involves private businesses, insurance companies, and consumers rather than only law enforcement agencies.

WHAT IS A FORENSIC ENTOMOLOGIST?

An *entomologist* is a scientist who studies insects; a *forensic entomologist* is the scientist who uses her expert knowledge of insects to help solve crimes and resolve legal disputes. A forensic entomologist must have many years of education and training before she can begin a career in crime-solving. She must complete four years of college or university and must have a master's of science program in entomology. Many forensic entomologists have a Ph.D., or doctor of philosophy, degree in entomology as well. To receive this degree, a forensic entomologist must complete five years of intensive study. During this time, she will specialize in an area of entomology that interests him, such as insects living in aquatic environments or insects useful in agriculture. Some forensic entomologists are medical doctors. These forensic entomologists must finish five years of medical school after college or university. Still other forensic entomologists specialize in *veterinary entomology*, the study of insects affecting the health of livestock and other animals, before beginning their careers. Most forensic entomologists work exclusively on medico-legal cases, so both an entomologist and a medical doctor who wish to become forensic entomologists study *medical entomology*, or the role of insects in human disease. Before she can practice forensic entomology,

however, a scientist must take a written test from the American Board of Forensic Entomology (ABFE), a professional organization that certifies forensic entomologists. The ABFE sets certain requirements for the education and experience a scientist must have to embark on a successful career in forensic entomology.

Many entomologists who receive certification to work on legal cases do not actually call themselves forensic entomologists. In fact, most "forensic entomologists" are entomologists with forensic training who teach and carry out their own research at colleges or universities. This group of scientists works on a limited number of cases each year because they must teach and conduct research, so they may not have as much

To practice forensic entomology, you must pass a written test administered by the American Board of Forensic Entomology.

NORTHERN ILLINOIS UNIVERSITY Testing Service

LAST NAME   INIT.   ID NUMBER   DEPT.   COURSE   DATE

Instructions: Using a softlead pencil, completely blacken only one oval per question. Do not use ink or colored pencil. Cleanly erase any unintended marks.

Poor / Good

MISC.   SEC.   FORM
A B C D E F

time to work on legal cases. A typical case may involve between five and fifteen hours of work in the laboratory, and some forensic entomologists participate in between fifteen and twenty cases each year. Few entomologists make a living working on legal cases alone, but some work independently, devoting their careers to forensic cases.

FROM LABORATORY TO COURTROOM

A forensic entomologist's job consists of two areas: the laboratory where she examines insect evidence and the courtroom where she presents her conclusions based on that evidence.

Forensic entomologists often divide their time between legal cases and their own research.

When a forensic entomologist begins work on a legal case, she first receives a request for her services from a law enforcement official. If she agrees to work on the case, law enforcement sends her crime-scene evidence, such as insects collected from a body and photographs of the crime scene. A forensic entomologist rarely visits a crime scene herself, so she must rely on crime-scene investigators, who are not entomologists, to carefully collect and preserve the insect evidence. Sometimes law enforcement agencies ask forensic entomologists to train crime-scene investigators to recognize and correctly collect and preserve insect evidence. This aspect of a forensic entomologist's job is important because she needs evidence that is as detailed and well preserved as possible in order to make accurate conclusions.

Insects collected from a crime scene usually arrive in carefully packaged parcels that protect them as they travel between the law enforcement agency and the forensic entomologist's laboratory. Once in the laboratory, a forensic entomologist reviews the crime-scene report and any photographs of the scene that might provide useful information about the insect specimens before examining the insects themselves. The most important information a forensic entomologist can determine from insect evidence is a victim's time of death. He estimates this period of time by identifying the different types and ages of the insects on the body. Many other factors, including the air temperature and humidity at the crime scene, help him calculate time of death as accurately as possible. He compares the time of death he expects from his estimate with the time of death other evidence in the case might indicate, such as the last time an eyewitness saw the victim alive. This helps him determine how accurate his estimate of time of death is and may also help him reveal crime-scene cover-ups and other interesting twists in a criminal case.

After examining the insect evidence in the laboratory, a forensic entomologist writes a report including her conclusions about the time of the victim's death, for example, and sends this report to a law enforcement official. If the case goes to court, she must testify as an expert witness, a professional who may give an opinion or conclusion about certain evidence because she has many years of experience and in-depth knowledge of the field in which she works. Testifying is the most difficult part of the job for many forensic entomologists because it requires speaking in front of a large audience and answering questions about her educational and career background, and even her personal life, which may be uncomfortable. A lawyer

As in other fields of forensics, entomologists are sometimes called to appear in court for their expert testimony.

CASE STUDY: BECOMING A PROMINENT FORENSIC ENTOMOLOGIST

When the Royal Canadian Mounted Police (RCMP) discovers insects at the scene of a homicide, they call on Dr. Gail Anderson, a board-certified forensic entomologist. As the only full-time forensic entomologist in Canada, Dr. Anderson rarely has a problem keeping busy. Not only does she work as a consultant on homicide cases for the RCMP, but she also consults for the British Columbia Coroner's Service and city police across Canada and abroad. When she is not cracking a criminal case, Dr. Anderson teaches forensic entomology at Simon Fraser University in British Columbia and lectures to law enforcement at the Canadian Police College.

In over fifteen years' experience in the field, Dr. Anderson has testified several times as an expert witness. She has been involved in cases from human murder to wildlife poaching, and as a highly respected scientist, her testimony can make or break an alibi and may help put a criminal behind bars.

To become a forensic entomologist, Dr. Anderson had to complete many years of school, finishing her training with a five-year Ph.D. in forensic entomology at Simon Fraser University. A scientist's education does not stop just because she has completed her degree, however. Dr. Anderson participates in many scientific societies such as the Canadian Society of Forensic Sciences and the Entomological

Society of Canada to keep abreast of current research and to share her work with other scientists.

Dr. Anderson's own research involves studying animal decomposition in different environments—from prairie forests to glacial pools. She especially wants to find a more accurate way of determining the time of death of victims found submerged in water, using the insects found on the victim's body. Working with colleagues and graduate students at Simon Fraser University, Dr. Anderson is currently compiling a database of forensically important insects across Canada. She has earned several awards for her outstanding contributions to forensic science and criminal justice.

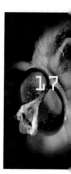

seeking to prove his client innocent of a crime asks these sorts of questions to make sure the forensic entomologist is experienced and competent, and that she made no mistakes when examining the evidence. Therefore, a forensic entomologist must keep a detailed record of her methods and observations in the laboratory so the jury will have no doubt about the credibility of her testimony. She also receives peer training before she testifies that prepares her for answering these types of questions.

To prove the validity of their findings in court, entomologists must keep detailed records of their studies and procedures.

A forensic entomologist's goal during a trial is to present the truth. Her testimony is powerful because a jury's decision may hinge upon the conclusions she draws from the insect evidence. Therefore, a forensic entomologist must describe her conclusions as clearly as possible in a way that the average person can understand. Her ability to communicate how she determined when and where the victim died, for example, is crucial because the jury uses this information to weigh the evidence for or against the defendant (person accused of a crime). The ability to bring justice through scientific work is one of the most rewarding aspects of the job for many forensic entomologists.

Despite the value of insect evidence, forensic entomologists are very new in the criminal justice system. In fact, Canada has just one full-time forensic entomologist (see case study on page 16). Only recently have forensic entomologists become a part of crime-scene investigation teams and crime labs in the United States and Canada; this is probably due to the fact that forensic entomology did not become a widespread field of study in North America until the mid-twentieth century. However, scientists in other parts of the world have been using insect evidence to solve crimes for nearly eight hundred years.

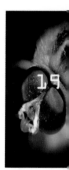

CHAPTER TWO

Forensic Entomology from East to West: A Natural History

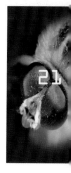

A forensic entomologist is no stranger to *maggots*—the close association between young flies and decomposing remains is the foundation of forensic entomology. Scientific writing, artwork, and theater over the past eight centuries open a window into the beginnings of forensic entomology because they reflect popular scientific knowledge during particular time periods.

EARLY BEGINNINGS IN THE EASTERN WORLD

Although forensic entomology is a relatively new scientific field in the Western world, scientists in the East have used insect evidence to solve crimes for hundreds of years. The oldest known case involving the forensic use of insects dates back to thirteenth-century China. In 1235, a lawyer and death investigator named Sung Tźu wrote a book titled *Hsi yüan chi lu* or *The Washing Away of Wrongs* (translated by McKnight, 1981).

In his book, Sung Tźu described a murder case in which flies revealed the man who committed the crime. The magistrate of the village in which Sung Tźu lived called all the

village workers to gather with their sickles so that he could question them about the body of a man found dead near a rice field. Slash wounds on the victim's body led the magistrate to suspect a worker in the rice field killed the man. Shortly after the workers arrived in front of the magistrate, flies began circling one worker's sickle in particular. Microscopic particles of dried blood and skin clinging to the sickle attracted the flies, which compelled the worker to confess to the murder.

The information Sung Tźu included in his textbook demonstrated early Eastern knowledge of insect behavior and biology. Not only did he include accounts of the cases he assisted, but he also described fly behavior on decomposing remains, the pattern in which they invaded different natural body openings, and different insects' attraction to wounds.

THE DANCES OF DEATH AND REDI'S FEAST OF MAGGOTS

Skeletons dance with smiling mouths agape, bony fingers beckoning the living to join in their *macabre* revelry. This is the scene depicted in *The Dances of Death*, a series of woodcuts from the fifteenth-century *medieval* period in Europe. The identity of the artists who crafted these woodcuts remains a mystery, but what historians do know about the artwork is that the Western world was familiar with the basic role of insects in human decomposition as early as the Middle Ages.

In *The Dances of Death*, maggots have already eaten the internal organs and cleaned the flesh from the skeletons' bones. Pieces of skin still remain, as do some of the maggots, which look more like small snakes. On some of the dancing corpses, only the head lacks flesh. The artists would have observed that the head is the first area of the body to lose flesh. Therefore, these woodcuts show that people in general associated maggots with decay and were familiar with the condition of decomposing corpses over time.

A second important piece of artwork is *Skeleton in the Tumba*, a detailed ivory carving from sixteenth-century Europe.

The sculpture depicts a corpse lying inside a coffin with some of its internal organs remaining. Maggots have nearly reduced the corpse to bones. (Decomposing corpses were common subjects for artists in premodern Europe when painters and sculptors could easily obtain a whole corpse or parts of one, explaining how artists could make such detailed observations of the human decomposition process.)

Written works are also useful for investigating how much the general population knew about the role of insects in decomposition. Around 1600, William Shakespeare tickled patrons of the Globe Theatre with *Hamlet* and other plays; people from many different walks of life could listen to one of his plays in the open-air theater. Shakespeare's witty references to maggots provide a glimpse into the general understanding of decay in early seventeenth-century England. That

The Dances of Death

"We fat all creatures else to fat us, and we fat ourselves for maggots."

—<u>Hamlet</u> Act IV (iii)

humans "fat themselves for maggots," or that maggots feed on corpses was common knowledge in Shakespeare's time.

The people of seventeenth-century Europe and North America stored their meat unrefrigerated. If meat was kept long enough, flies eventually followed its strong odor, and maggots appeared on the meat. Someone in the twenty-first century would probably assume that the flies circling the meat a few days before had laid their eggs in it. After all, meat provides hungry fly larvae with a convenient, nutritious food source and a safe place to grow and develop. However, a person living in seventeenth-century Europe or North America would probably come to a very different conclusion.

Four hundred years ago, popular belief was that rotting meat actually produced maggots, and people in general made no connection between the flies they saw on meat and the maggots that soon followed. Hamlet's quip, "For if the sun breed maggots in a dead dog, being a kissing carrion," is an excellent example of this seventeenth-century belief. The hypothesis that rotting meat suddenly created maggots was called *spontaneous generation*. The disproof of this hypothesis laid the early foundation for the science of forensic entomology.

In 1668, an Italian scientist named Francesco Redi (1626–1698) changed the way the Western world thought about maggots. At this time, the idea that maggots were actually young flies was still unheard of in the West, and so the

Francesco Redi

goal of Redi's experiments was to collect empirical evidence to discover how and why maggots appeared on rotting meat. (Empirical evidence is one or more observations a scientist makes with his senses of sight, smell, taste, hearing, or touch. He uses these observations to support or disprove a hypothesis.)

Redi designed a *controlled experiment* in which he compared meat left out in the open air and exposed to flies with meat that he covered and protected from flies. No maggots appeared on the covered meat, but the uncovered meat attracted

Maggots can hatch from eggs laid on unrefrigerated or uncovered meat.

flies that quickly laid eggs in the soft, moist tissue. When maggots emerged from the eggs, Redi concluded that rotting meat did not produce maggots; on the contrary, maggots were young flies!

METAMORPHOSIS

Most of the early writing on the use of insect evidence in legal proceedings came from Europe, and physicians were often the scientists who examined crime-scene evidence. Nearly two hundred years after Redi's experiments, Bergeret d'Arbois, a French physician, was the first scientist to publish methods for estimating *postmortem interval* (PMI). He used the developmental stages of insects on a corpse to estimate a victim's time of death.

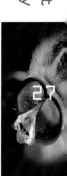

Maggots grow into adult flies.

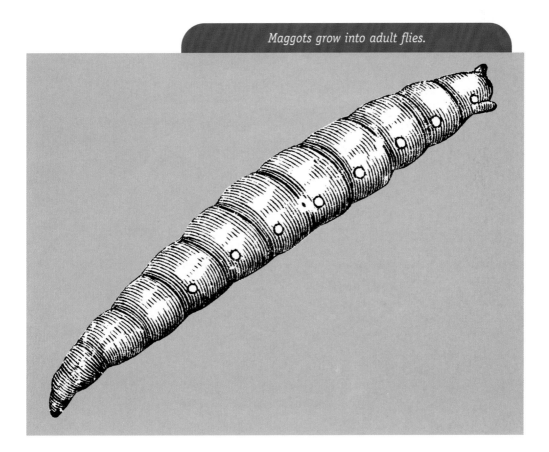

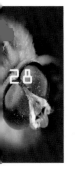

Bergeret's case involved the discovery of an infant's mummified corpse behind a fireplace. "What was the time interval between birth and death?" he wrote in his 1855 publication. "To answer this question, legal medicine must check with another science, the Natural Sciences." On the body, Bergeret found moths in their first stages of development, as well as flesh flies (Musca carnaria) and the cases in which they developed into adults. Since he believed *metamorphosis*, the development of a maggot into an adult fly, took one year, he concluded the two generations of insects indicated the body found in 1850 had died in 1848. The flesh fly laid eggs in 1848 while the body was still fresh, but the moth laid eggs on the dry corpse in 1849. Bergeret presented this evidence in front of a

An adult fly

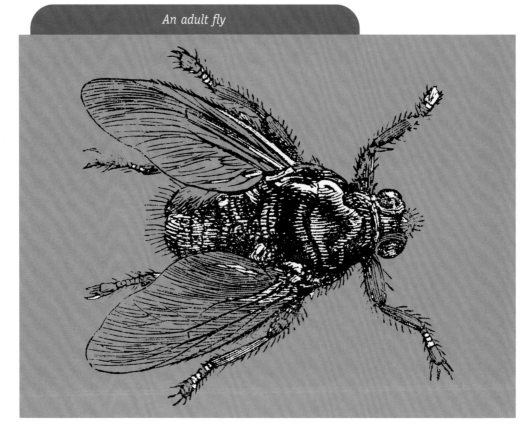

magistrate, stating the previous tenants of the house, not the present inhabitants, were most likely guilty of the crime.

Jean Pierre Mégnin published the first report on the predictable pattern in which insects invade corpses. A French Army veterinarian, Mégnin wrote a book on his succession theory in 1894 titled, *La Faune des Cadavres*, or *The Fauna on Cadavres*. According to his theory, decomposing bodies underwent eight stages of insect infestation when exposed to the outdoor environment and only two stages when buried in soil. Drawings of insects and other animals commonly found on or

A moth

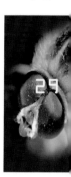

near decaying remains accompanied descriptions of cases he assisted as a scientist and expert witness. Mégnin's book contributed valuable knowledge to the study of animals and plants useful to forensics.

The depth of research in North America increased in the 1950s and 1960s with Bernard Greenberg's studies on the biology and reproduction of many insect species important to forensic entomology. Jerry Payne carried out decomposition studies on pig carcasses to research different stages of insect colonization on decaying remains. In his article, "A summer

Scientists use pigs in their research to mirror the effects of human decomposition.

carrion study of the baby pig *Sus scrofa* Linnaeus," Payne described over five hundred kinds of insects and six decomposition stages forensic entomologists can use to estimate a victim's time and place of death.

ADVANCES IN TAXONOMY

Taxonomy, the science of classifying and naming living things, plays a critical role in forensic entomology. Forensic entomologists must identify the insects on a body before they can analyze the location and time of death. Once a forensic entomologist identifies which kinds of insects are on the corpse, he can find out the behavior of these insects on a decaying body, the geographic locations where these insects occur, and how long development from maggot to adult takes. He needs all this information to determine where and when the victim died. However, taxonomists only began studying insects useful to forensics in the early twentieth century.

Several North American entomologists in the first half of the twentieth century illustrated important insects such as flesh fly and blowfly maggots and adults. Descriptions of the insects' physical features and biology often accompanied these drawings. Together, the sketches and descriptions served as early identification tools. Many insect guidebooks now contain detailed photographs that are most helpful in correctly identifying adult flies, among other insects. However, identifying fly maggots is very difficult, and sometimes a forensic entomologist needs to be able to accurately tell one maggot from another to solve a case. Today, high-powered microscopes make the process a little easier because forensic entomologists can view tiny, unique features of young fly maggots and the cases in which they finish developing into adult flies. Scientists and students at colleges and universities continue to develop new techniques for identifying insects in their early stages of development.

FORENSIC ENTOMOLOGY TODAY

Today, an increasing number of forensic entomologists make up medical and legal investigation teams at crime scenes and in laboratories. Entomologists can join many organizations that give them a place to exchange information and ideas. In 1996, a small group of entomologists who mainly work on criminal cases formed the ABFE. Professional organizations such as the ABFE set scientific, ethical, and educational standards for entomologists who practice or plan to practice forensic work. These organizations also connect them to scientists with similar interests the world over. Other professional organizations to which forensic entomologists belong include the American

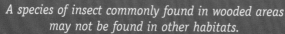

A species of insect commonly found in wooded areas may not be found in other habitats.

Registry of Professional Entomologists and the American Academy of Forensic Sciences.

Research in forensic entomology at North American universities such as Simon Fraser University in British Columbia, Texas A&M University, and the University of Missouri–Columbia continues to expand with studies of insect growth and development in different climates, insect behavior on carcasses, the geographic locations where different insects occur, and the decomposition process in diverse *habitat* types. Over the past thirty years, more and more entomologists have begun doing research specifically for forensic purposes. Forensic entomology continues to gain professional, academic, and popular interest in North America, Europe, South Africa, Australia, and many other parts of the world.

This research is critical to a forensic entomologist's ability to provide law enforcement with a victim's time of death in criminal cases, and to estimate the source and timing of infestations in food, textiles, and other items in *civil* cases. The way forensic entomologists estimate a person's time of death using insect evidence is perhaps the most fascinating aspect of forensic entomology, and is based on many years of studying some interesting subjects—including pigs in human clothing.

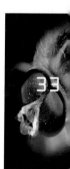

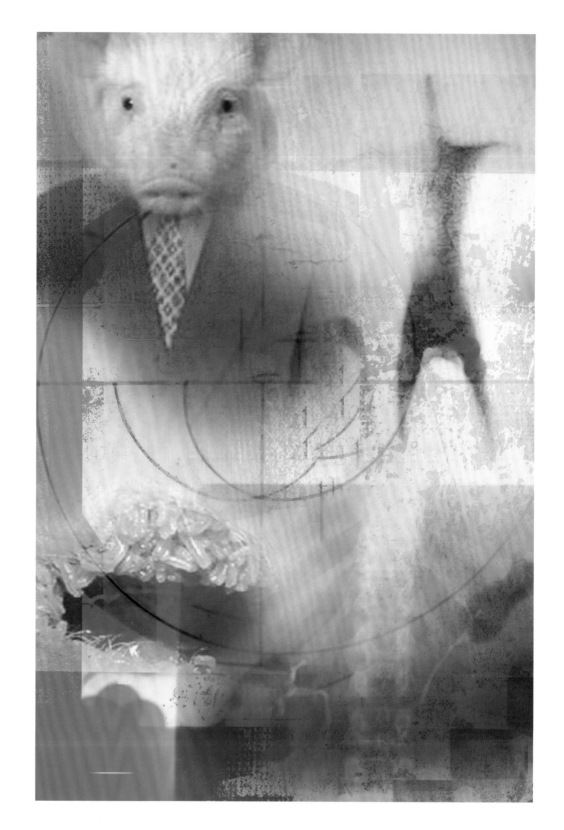

CHAPTER THREE

Bodies, Blowflies, and Pigs in Clothing

Bodies

decompose at various depths in the icy cold water. A person out for a weekend stroll might be alarmed to stumble upon such a scene, but for the Niagara Police in Ontario, these bodies are just another part of crime-solving.

The bodies are not actually human bodies but the carcasses of pigs dressed in human clothing. By periodically weighing the carcasses and collecting insects from them, the Niagara Police will find out how bodies decompose in very cold fresh-water environments, and the kinds of insects that feed on them. Hopefully, these pigs in human clothing will bring law enforcement in Canada and the United States one step closer to finding out when a victim submerged in glacial water died.

Insects on a victim or suspect and elsewhere at a crime scene help forensic entomologists determine when and where a victim died. In the case at the start of this book, the grasshopper linked the suspect to the victim at the crime scene, but law enforcement agencies most often ask forensic entomologists to estimate a victim's time and place of death. To do this, forensic entomologists must have expert knowledge of insect

biology and behavior, such as the habitat, temperature, and climate different insects prefer for egg laying, hatching, and growth.

Forensic entomologists use two biological concepts, *succession*—the pattern in which different groups of insects invade a corpse—and *life cycle*, or the stages of insect growth and development, to find out when and where a victim died. Insects may be small, but their complex world tells scientists stories that can make or break a criminal case.

THE BODY AS AN ISLAND

Insects are the most abundant animals on Earth in terms of the number of different kinds or species and the sheer number of individuals. An estimated 900,000 known insect species fly, crawl, and swim about our world, but no one really knows how many species exist because there are too many to count! Insects live in a diverse array of habitats and climates. They are almost everywhere, making them excellent forensic tools. Two groups of insects, flies (*Diptera*) and beetles (*Coleoptera*), are especially important to forensic entomologists because they are the most common insects on decaying remains in many different habitats and climates.

Forensic entomologists think of a body as a temporary microhabitat, or a small patch of habitat with a slightly different climate and insect community than the larger living environment to which the body belongs. The body goes through changes in temperature and moisture as it decomposes, making it hospitable to different kinds of insects at different times. Which insects live on or near the body depends on their requirements for food, climate, and shelter. Insects invade the body in a generally predictable pattern, although this succession does vary between regions as climate, habitat, and insect species change. For example, bodies stay moist and attractive to flies much longer in humid tropical regions than in dry deserts. Similarly, beetles that usually eat dry remains in *tem-*

perate climates are absent from corpses in the tropics because the corpse does not dry.

Flies arrive at a decomposing body first. Blowflies (family *Calliphoridae*) and flesh flies (family *Sarcophagidae*) are the most common types of flies forensic entomologists find on a body. This is probably because decomposing remains give flies and their young a protein-rich food to eat as well as an excellent place to breed.

Communities of insects may inhabit a human body in decay.

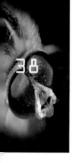

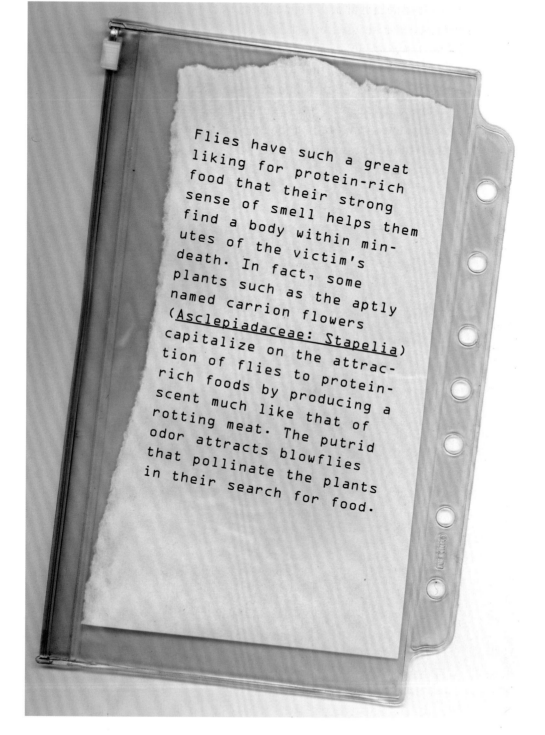

Flies have such a great liking for protein-rich food that their strong sense of smell helps them find a body within minutes of the victim's death. In fact, some plants such as the aptly named carrion flowers (<u>Asclepiadaceae: Stapelia</u>) capitalize on the attraction of flies to protein-rich foods by producing a scent much like that of rotting meat. The putrid odor attracts blowflies that pollinate the plants in their search for food.

On a decomposing body, flies drink blood and other fluids to give them energy to breed. Blowflies lay eggs in natural body openings. Twelve to eighteen hours later, the larvae (singular: *larva*), commonly known as maggots, emerge from their eggs to find themselves on a great expanse of food. Flesh flies have a different strategy, however. These flies give birth to live larvae and drop them into body openings as they fly past. As eggs and larvae multiply, ants and *predatory* beetles carry some away and eat them.

Soon the body heats up because more and larger larvae quickly consume great amounts of flesh—and the body's natural bacteria begin breaking down tissues as well, adding more

Beetles prey on fly eggs and larvae.

heat. Temperatures inside the body may reach 127 degrees Fahrenheit (53 degrees Celsius). Given enough time, multiple generations of flies can live off the body. As the body slowly dries and leaves little food for maggots, hister beetles (family *Histeridae*), rove beetles (family *Staphylinidae*), and burying beetles (family *Silphidae*), among others, feed on the body where it meets the soil. These beetles eat maggots when they are plentiful but only eat flesh when it is dry.

The activity of all these creatures will cause changes in the soil. Fly larvae have special hooks on their mouths for tearing flesh, but before they can eat a morsel of this food, they first need to soften it. The larvae spit a fluid containing enzymes, proteins that break up food and other substances, onto the

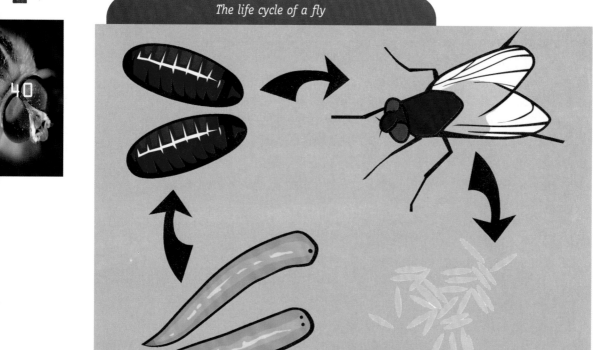

The life cycle of a fly

flesh to soften it until it is nearly a liquid. This process releases ammonia, which soaks into the soil. Insects that cannot tolerate this chemical leave the soil, while others who benefit from it move in. The change in the soil beneath a body is often so dramatic that decay-loving insects stay in the soil years after a body has been removed.

To make the "creature-scape" even more complicated, some insects move in to eat the other insects on the body. Large numbers of fly larvae attract predators such as beetles and ants. Wasps lay their eggs in fly larvae. Eventually, maggots stop eating and move away from the body to a drier environment in which to finish developing into adult flies. Insects that survive on decomposing flesh leave the body when only bones and hair remain. Over time, the "island" that provided such a rich, protected food source for a diverse assembly of insects sinks into the soil.

INSECT DEVELOPMENT

Forensic entomologists most often use flies to estimate a victim's time of death. Flies have a *holometabolous* life cycle, meaning the fly's appearance in its larval stages is radically different from its appearance in its adult stage. This is one of the qualities that makes flies excellent tools for forensic investigation. Flies go through six stages of development:

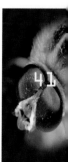

- egg
- first instar larva
- second instar larva
- third instar larva
- pupa
- adult

Eggs of different fly species hatch at different times, depending on the temperature of their environment. When they hatch, a first instar larva emerges. (An instar is a stage of larval development.) A larva goes through changes in physical

features during each instar. These changes can be so subtle and may involve such tiny features that instars are hard to identify without a microscope. Inside the pupa (a protective casing of spun silk, leaves, or other materials from the environment), the larva develops into an adult fly.

The amount of time a fly takes to grow from one stage to the next depends mainly on temperature. In general, flies develop from egg to adult in ten to twenty-seven days at 80 degrees Fahrenheit (27 degrees Celsius). Insects are vulnerable to extreme heat and cold because they cannot regulate their own body temperature. If temperatures become either too hot or too cold, flies will not fly or lay eggs, and larvae will not grow. A decrease in temperature by 50 degrees Fahrenheit (10 degrees Celsius) can significantly slow larval growth. The temperatures that support *metabolic* function are unique to each fly species and allow them to live in different geographic locations, seasons, and climates. For this reason, different types of insects invade decomposing remains in different regions of the world.

WHEN DID THE CRIME HAPPEN?

The period between the victim's death and the discovery of his body is the PMI. Forensic entomologists record the age, or development stage, of the insects on the body to find out when insects first arrived at the remains. Because flies locate a decomposing body within minutes of the victim's death, the age of flies on the body is pretty close to the PMI in most cases.

To find out how old the flies are, forensic entomologists need to know what the temperatures were at the crime scene during the suspected time of death, the species of flies on the body, how old these flies are, and how many generations of flies developed on the body. A weather station close to the location of the body can usually give forensic entomologists the climate information they need. If not, the National Oceanic and Atmospheric Administration (NOAA) is a good source of weather information.

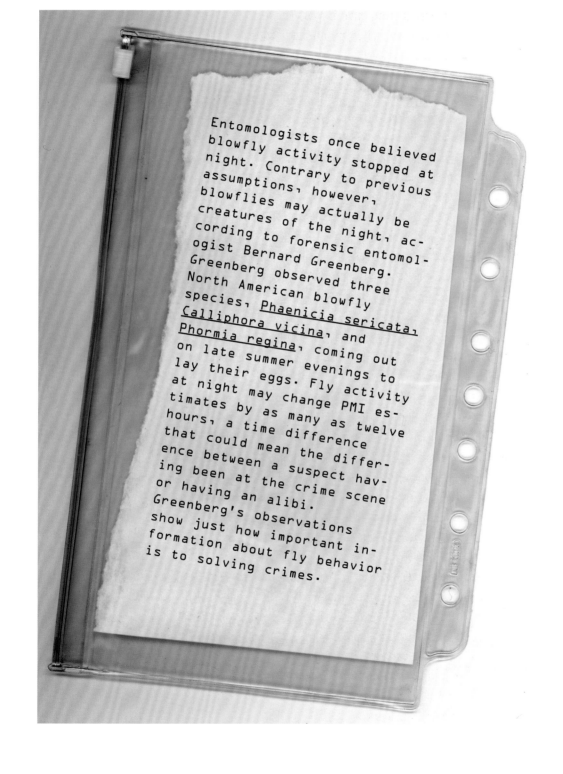

Entomologists once believed blowfly activity stopped at night. Contrary to previous assumptions, however, blowflies may actually be creatures of the night, according to forensic entomologist Bernard Greenberg. Greenberg observed three North American blowfly species, _Phaenicia sericata_, _Calliphora vicina_, and _Phormia regina_, coming out on late summer evenings to lay their eggs. Fly activity at night may change PMI estimates by as many as twelve hours, a time difference that could mean the difference between a suspect having been at the crime scene or having an alibi. Greenberg's observations show just how important information about fly behavior is to solving crimes.

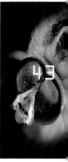

44

CASE STUDY: GROWING DEAD BODIES

"The Body Farm" is a famous research facility where scientists study the decomposition of human remains. William Bass, a forensic anthropologist, started the body farm in 1971 at the University of Tennessee Medical Center in Knoxville. Very little research on human decomposition existed before Bass started the facility. Today, nearly forty bodies in various situations—buried under brush, in ponds, and in shallow graves—decompose on this plot of land at one time. The bodies come from personal donations or from local morgues if no one claims the bodies. Research on the farm has contributed to estimating time of death by comparing human decomposition and insect succession on human bodies in a variety of environments and scenarios. Particularly important to law enforcement are studies of covered or buried bodies. A criminal's attempt to hide a body may also protect it from insects, which influences the PMI estimate because insects may not be able to invade the body until days after the victim's death. The Body Farm is in fact so well known that even agents from the Federal Bureau of Investigation (FBI) use it to simulate such crime scenes.

On a much smaller scale, some forensic entomologists use a pig carcass in human clothing to study decomposition. The decomposition of a pig carcass closely resembles that of a human body and is not as alarming to someone who might jog by it on a sunny day. The goal of any decomposition study is to find the most precise way to estimate PMI. Decomposition studies provide forensic entomologists with information about what species of insects occur at different stages of decomposition in a given environment. For example, if a forensic entomologist wants to observe when different types of insects invade a body in a dense forest at the height of summer, he will return to collect insects from the pig carcass and the soil around it throughout its decomposition, recording the insects' developmental stages. He will also record changes in the environment around the pig, such as humidity, temperature, and rainfall. He can compare the data he collects with similar real-life cases to determine PMI.

Identifying the species of flies on the body is important because different species grow and develop at different rates, depending on the temperature of their environment. The growth information helps forensic scientists figure out how old the flies are once they know the flies' development stages. Comparing the known development stage of flies on the corpse with how long laboratory flies of the same species took to reach that stage at a known temperature helps forensic entomologists estimate the age of the flies. However, the temperature at the crime scene is rarely constant. Forensic entomologists average temperature data over the number of days since the suspected time of death. They can then calculate the time the insects on the body needed to reach certain development

By studying the temperatures of insect habitats, scientists can chart which species have nested in a body, and gain clues to the victim's time of death.

stages at an average crime-scene temperature. If multiple fly generations lived on the body, forensic entomologists must add together the development times from the different generations. The development time of the oldest flies, in numbers of days or hours, is approximate to the PMI.

The longer a victim has been dead, the less accurate estimates of PMI become because many generations of flies colonize a body in a short period of time, and eventually the maggots, the most useful of the development stages, grow into adulthood and fly away. This situation leaves forensic entomologists with little evidence for estimating the PMI.

For example, a PMI estimate for a victim in Washington, D.C., was three days shorter than the victim's actual time of death because so little insect evidence remained on the body. Photographs of the body showed some maggots almost ready to pupate. They had begun moving away from the body to find a dry place to do so. It was November, so the cold may have caused these maggots to develop more slowly than usual. Given the time these few maggots should have taken to develop through their third instar and the cold November temperatures, the PMI would have been fifteen days. However, later evidence in the case proved the crime took place eighteen days before authorities discovered the body. Furthermore, the suspect had moved the body from the crime scene and buried it in debris, which may have prevented the insects from invading the body for a few days.

WHERE DID THE CRIME HAPPEN?

The ways insects interact with the world around them can give investigators clues about the location of the crime scene. In some cases, criminals move the body to a different location to hide the scene and any evidence that might lead to their capture. The geographic range and habitat of certain insect species can reveal whether or not the suspect moved the body. If a suspect transports a victim from a city to a forest, forest-dwelling insects should invade the body. But also, an "urban" insect

CASE STUDY: BLOWFLY CLUES

Blowflies led authorities in Illinois to a hidden crime scene because these flies make no secret of their love for decaying remains. The only clue authorities had was that someone had thrown a body down a well on a farm. Illinois has many farms, so this clue was not very helpful. Authorities drove through the plains searching every well they could find. A dark cloud of flies circling the well at one of the farms gave away the crime scene. The suspect had covered the hole with old tires, protecting the victim's body from the flies. Authorities could thank the flies and their strong sense of smell for helping them find the crime scene.

species that typically lives in buildings might be expected to come crawling out of the victim's hat. This insect would have clung to the victim on the way from the city to the forest.

Looking for the unexpected is something that forensic entomologists do best. Comparing what kinds of insects they expect to be on the body with the kinds of insects they observe on the body helps alert a forensic entomologist to important clues.

WHO COMMITTED THE CRIME?

In the early summer of 1989, scuba divers came upon a car submerged in the Muskegon River in western Michigan. The car

Entomological evidence can reveal whether a body has been moved from an urban area to a rural one.

contained the body of a woman. Police discovered the car belonged to the woman's husband, and the *medical examiner* found injuries to the woman's head that could not have been caused by a car accident. Based on this and other evidence, authorities suspected her husband of murder.

However, her husband insisted he argued with his wife a few weeks before the divers discovered her body and that she had driven away in his car on the night of the argument. He claimed he had not heard from her since then. Because the car did not look like it had crashed into the water, police were reluctant to believe his story.

Unfortunately, the cold water preserved the woman's body so that estimating PMI proved too difficult. Crime-scene detectives collected aquatic insects (insects that spend part or all of

When there are no other witnesses, insects may hold the most information about a crime.

their lives in water) from the windshield, fender, and door handles of the car, hoping an entomologist would be able to determine when the car first rolled into the river. This point in time would represent the woman's time of death.

Richard Merritt, an aquatic entomologist who works at Michigan State University, identified caddisfly cases, chironomid beetle larvae (family *Chironomidae*), and blackfly larvae and pupae of the genus *Praimulium*. He used the life cycle of these blackflies to estimate PMI. The blackflies he examined lay eggs in late spring and early summer, but the eggs hatch

Aquatic insects provide forensic entomologists with clues.

CASE STUDY: USING A MICROSCOPE
TO GET TO KNOW INSECTS

Identifying fly larvae may be one of the most challenging and tedious tasks a forensic entomologist faces. That's why the microscope is an important tool in the forensic entomologist's laboratory—it helps him identify insect larvae collected from a crime scene. If a forensic entomologist wants to determine the age of an insect larva collected from a body, for example, he must find out the species of the insect larva, because different types of insects grow and develop at different rates. Just knowing that the insects are flies will not give him a precise estimate of a victim's time of death. He must know what kinds of flies fed on the victim in order to provide a useful estimate of PMI. With the aid of a microscope, a forensic entomologist can examine certain physical characteristics that are unique to each species of insect larvae but too small to view with the naked eye. For instance, the body openings through which fly larvae breathe, called spiracles, distinguish one species of fly larva from another. A forensic entomologist looks at the shape and size of these openings under a microscope to determine the species of fly larva before he begins calculating the age of the larvae. Occasionally, when two species are too similar to be distinguished from each other under a low- powered microscope, he must look at the spiracles in such detail that he uses a very powerful microscope called a scanning electron microscope (SEM). A beam of electrons scans the surface of the larva to provide a finely detailed image of the spiracles.

in river- and streambed sediments in the late fall or early winter of the next year. The larvae then attach to surfaces such as rocks or vegetation, where they grow very slowly during the cold winter months. The blackflies in this case attached to the woman's car. In March or April, the larvae pupate, emerging from their cocoons in early to mid-May. Adult blackflies feed on blood to gain enough energy for mating and egg-laying. The flies die one or two months later. Dr. Merritt then identified the species of blackfly from the pupal cases to determine how long each development stage would have taken, and from this made a more exact estimate of PMI.

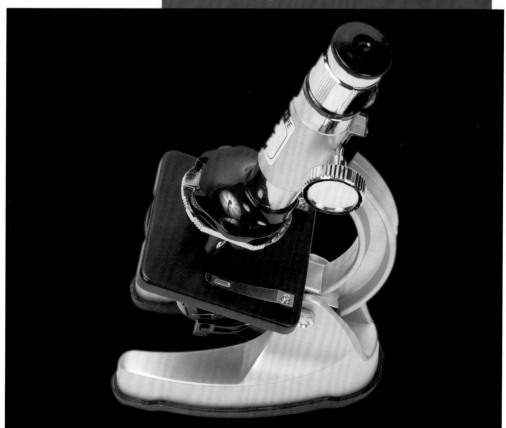

Entomologists conduct most of their research in the lab, not at the crime scene.

Based on the time of year this particular species of black-fly larvae attach to a surface to pupate, Dr. Merritt concluded the car must have gone into the water nine months before the discovery of the woman's body, during the previous winter. The life cycle of a single insect proved the husband was lying about the time of his wife's disappearance. She had in fact disappeared in the fall of 1988. This and other evidence helped link him to the murder of his wife. A jury convicted him of second-degree murder, and he is now serving a life sentence in prison.

DRUGS AND TOXINS IN MEDICO-LEGAL FORENSIC ENTOMOLOGY

Sometimes a body has very little tissue left, so directly measuring the amounts of drugs or toxins in the victim's system is impossible. An indirect way of finding out if toxic or illegal substances played a role in a person's death is to sample the tissues of maggots found on or near the body. If maggots feed on the remains of someone who has taken drugs or ingested poison, these maggots will also contain that chemical.

The effects of drugs and toxins on insect growth are important to estimating PMI. For example, drugs such as cocaine increase the growth rate of maggots. This information is useful because a forensic entomologist calculates the PMI by measuring the body length of maggots collected from a body. Body length, in addition to development stage, can indicate the age of the maggots. If human tissues contain a phagostimulant, a drug or toxin that increases the rate at which maggots feed, large maggots may still be young maggots, just overfed. In *A Fly for the Prosecution: How Insect Evidence Helps Solve Crimes*, forensic entomologist M. Lee Goff described two cases in which his understanding of drugs and toxins helped him find out the cause and time of death.

In 1980, a twenty-year-old woman was found in a creek bed. Beside her lay a pocketbook containing an empty bottle with a prescription for one hundred tablets of phenobarbital, a potentially lethal drug, which indicated the drug had been involved in her death. Unfortunately, very little tissue remained that could be analyzed for drugs or toxins. However, maggots of a blowfly species still fed on the body. Results of a toxicology analysis—an analysis of all the foreign chemicals present in bodily tissues and fluids—showed the maggots feeding on the corpse were full of phenobarbital.

Another challenging case in 1987 required Goff to use an understanding of insect life cycles and the affect of drugs on insect growth to find the time and cause of death of a fifty-

Toxicology analysis led investigators to conclude the victim had been poisoned.

eight-year-old man. A bottle of the insecticide Malathion, of which one-quarter of the liquid was missing, lay next to the corpse. Goff suspected the man died after drinking the Malathion. Goff noticed some maggots on the body were in their late third instar, but others were in their second instar. He raised the maggots in the laboratory until they developed into adults. Goff saw the maggots belonged to two blowfly species, *Chrysomya megacephala* and *Chrysomya rufifacies*. He found maggots of the former species in the third instar and those of the latter species in both the second and third instar. Using his knowledge of the number of days each fly species took to develop into these instars under the air temperature at

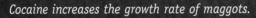

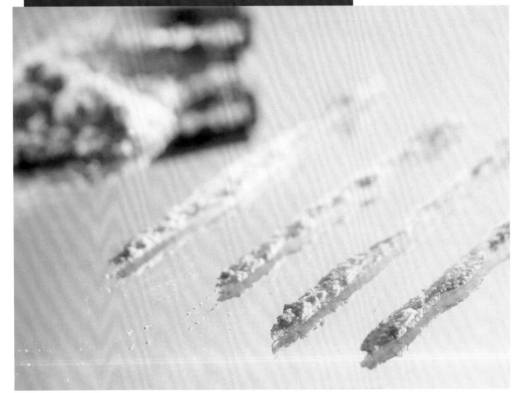

Cocaine increases the growth rate of maggots.

CASE STUDY: MAGGOTS AND COCAINE

In 1988, research on the influence of cocaine on
fly development helped solve a murder case in
Spokane, Washington, after authorities had discovered the body of a young woman lying face down in
a pine clearing. Unexpectedly large maggots 17 to
18 millimeters (less than an inch) long fed in the
corpse's nose, but only small maggots 6 to 9 millimeters or shorter fed on the rest of the body.
Given the maggots—larvae of two blowfly species
(<u>Phaenicia sericata</u> and <u>Cynomyopsis cadaverina</u>)—
took about three weeks to reach 17 or 18 millimeters, but only seven days to grow to between 6 and
9 millimeters, something was out of the ordinary.
Other evidence in the case ruled out a three-week
PMI, so what explained the unusually large maggots? The key was the woman's habit: not only did
she abuse cocaine, she inhaled it through her
nose. Since cocaine increases the rate of maggot
growth, the largest maggots would be located in
the corpse's nose, which contained the highest
levels of cocaine. To find out how old the largest
maggots actually were, the forensic entomologist
needed to know how fast these maggots grew on a
near-lethal cocaine diet. Comparing the largest
maggots' growth rate with the growth rate of
cocaine-fed maggots in the laboratory revealed
the woman died seven days before authorities
arrived at the crime scene.

57

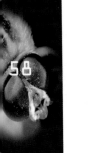

which he found the corpse, Goff estimated that the man died five days before investigators discovered his body.

Complications arose when Goff considered the receipt found on the bottle of Malathion, which showed the man bought the insecticide eight days before his death. Furthermore, a witness reported seeing the man alive eight days before the discovery of the corpse. Forensic entomologists use the last time a victim was seen alive to help estimate PMI. The time of death the insect evidence predicted did not match the time of death the eyewitness and the receipt indicated.

When Goff compared the number of insect species on the body with the number of species he expected to find, he no-

Malathion is a poison used to kill insects.

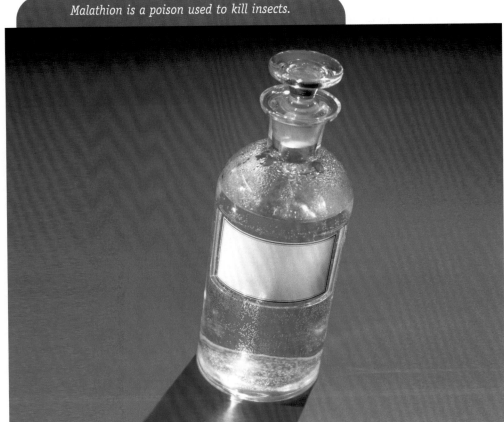

ticed something else was amiss: insects were missing! According to data from his decomposition studies, more species of insects such as the common housefly (*Musca domestica*) and species of hide beetles (family *Dermestidae*) should have invaded the body by the time of its discovery if indeed the body was exposed to insects for eight days.

More intriguing still was the fact that most of the maggots found on the body fed on the mouth area, which was an unexpected occurrence because the man drank a highly potent insecticide. Puzzled, Goff took these maggots to the laboratory for toxicology analysis and discovered surprisingly high levels of the insecticide in their tissue, so high that adult flies could not have survived such a dose.

How did the adult flies survive after consuming the poisoned flesh? In the laboratory, the maggots developed to their adult stage under dosages of the insecticide toxic to adult flies. The adult flies at the crime scene would have survived and continued to lay eggs because adult houseflies do not feed directly on flesh. As the maggots fed, the Malathion in the flesh broke down, so that over time the flesh grew less toxic and other species of insects could tolerate eating it. Goff suspected this process took three days, after which the usual pattern of insect succession would resume, explaining the absence of certain insect species and conflicting predictions of PMI. Investigators most likely arrived at the scene before other species could colonize the body.

59

FLYSPECKS

Insect evidence may help crime-scene investigators reconstruct the sequence of events of a crime. However, in some cases the very insects that play a valuable role in solving a crime can also complicate the problem-solving process and may even at first lead crime scene investigators to incorrect conclusions. For example, blood spatter on walls or other surfaces at a crime scene usually indicates a violent injury took place, but flies feeding on blood from human injuries may also leave numerous similar

CASE STUDY: FLYSPECKS AND MURDER

In 1997, a double homicide in a Lincoln, Nebraska,
apartment shocked forensics specialists investigating the scene because blood spots of a broad size
range occurred on numerous surfaces in almost
every room and in random patterns. Spots ranged in
size from those typical of low- to high-impact velocity injuries consistent with gunshot wounds.
Because of the random distribution and inconclusive origin of some of the blood spots, investigators at first believed the humans involved in the
crime struggled with an intruder while moving
about the entire apartment before dying of gunshot
wounds. The motivation for the crime pointed to
burglary or assault.

Insect evidence from the bodies consisted of
adult black blowflies (<u>Phormia regina</u>) and their
first- and third-instar larvae. The flies laid
eggs in two distinct egg-laying periods evidenced
by the small size of the first instar larvae and
the significantly larger size of larvae in the
third instar. In addition to laying eggs, the
adult flies fed on blood from the bodies. The un-
usual blood spots were most likely remnants of regurgitated blood meals or defecation from feeding
flies.

Dr. Benecke and Dr. Barksdale tested this hypothesis in the laboratory by feeding adult black
blowflies a reddish-brown-colored food and observ-
ing the shape, size, and distribution of stains

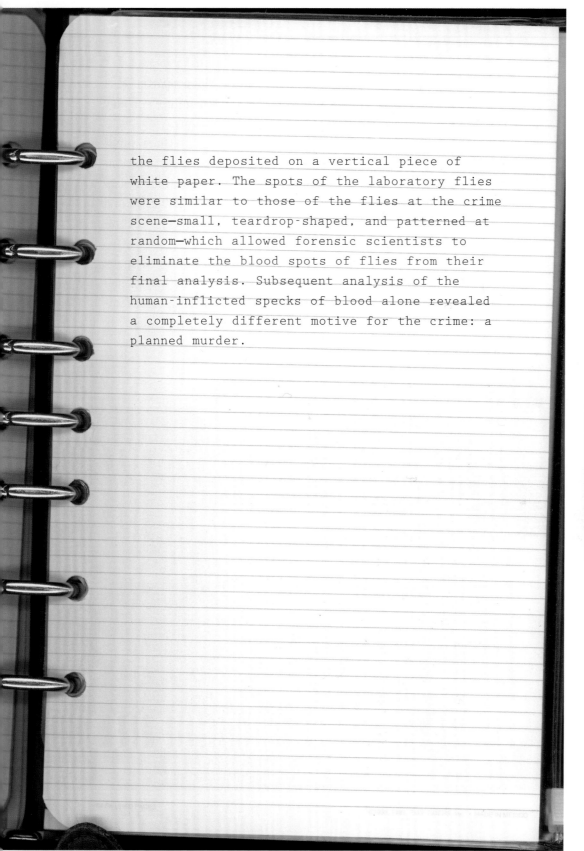

the flies deposited on a vertical piece of white paper. The spots of the laboratory flies were similar to those of the flies at the crime scene—small, teardrop-shaped, and patterned at random—which allowed forensic scientists to eliminate the blood spots of flies from their final analysis. Subsequent analysis of the human-inflicted specks of blood alone revealed a completely different motive for the crime: a planned murder.

blood spots in the same locations. Thus, blood spatter at a crime scene may originate solely from human injuries or may contain a mixture of stains from flies and humans.

Flies leave blood spots at a crime scene in three ways: vomiting blood onto a surface, defecating blood after consuming it, and landing on a surface after resting on blood elsewhere in the crime scene. Entomologists Mark Benecke and Larry Barksdale recently described ways crime-scene technicians can recognize such "flyspecks."

The physical characteristics, shape and size of blood spots, and their location and angle relative to a body may help crime-scene technicians and other specialists identify flyspecks. Tear-shaped or symmetrically round blood specks with "craters" in

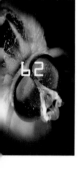

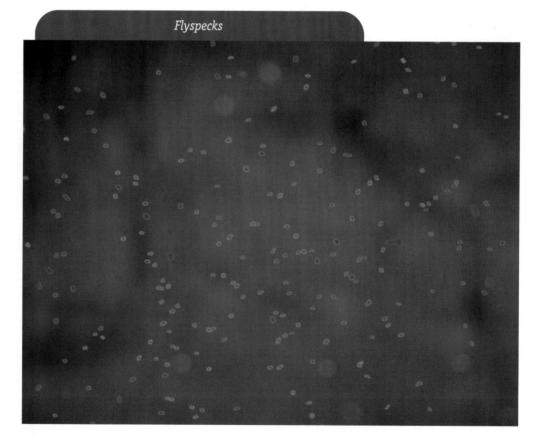

Flyspecks

the center, distributed in a random pattern, distinguish blood remnants typical of the common housefly.

Recognizing flyspecks requires some knowledge of the feeding behavior of different species of flies. Shortly after consuming blood, a fly regurgitates it onto a surface such as a wall or ceiling, or the body and clothes of a corpse. Enzymes in the fly's saliva predigest the portion of blood that the fly then laps or sucks up. When a common housefly sucks up blood, its proboscis—the tubular, sucking organ with which it eats—leaves a crater in the blood spot. Crime-scene investigators can use

After consuming blood, insects will often regurgitate or defecate it onto another location at a crime scene.

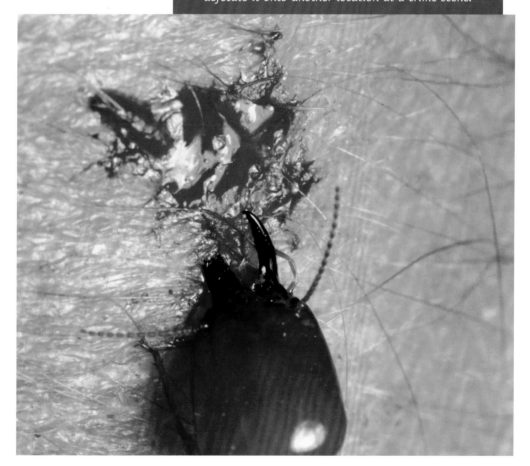

this characteristic to recognize the blood specks these flies leave after feeding.

The shape and size of blood spots may distinguish flyspecks from human-inflicted blood spots, because flies defecating blood onto surfaces at a crime scene tend to leave teardropshaped stains or small, symmetrically round stains, usually smeared when flies evacuate blood by-products while flying over a surface. Spots of regurgitated or defecated blood may be as small as one millimeter in diameter, about the same size as blood spots consistent with a low-impact *velocity injury*. Blood spots from a single human-inflicted injury originate from the same location in the crime scene and usually occur in a distinct pattern dependent on the cause of injury. Dr. Benecke and Dr.

Different patterns of blood spatter

Barksdale discovered that flyspecks occur in most areas of a crime scene and in a random pattern. Due to the random distribution of these blood spots, calculations of the angle between a body and blood spots nearby will give conflicting results—each blood spot will show the blood spattered on the surface came from a different direction. Therefore, crime-scene investigators must identify and eliminate flyspecks from their analyses in order to determine the correct location and cause of injury or death.

Forensic entomologists help law enforcement determine when and where a victim died by looking at the number and kinds of insects on the victim's body, the development stage of these insects, and their life cycles. The clues forensic entomologists are able to glean from insects at a crime scene depend on decades of laboratory research into insect growth and development and the decomposition of remains in different environments. Every case gives forensic entomologists new information about insect behavior that may help solve future crimes. In this way, insects not only provide silent witnesses for the dead but also help protect the living.

Most of the cases forensic entomologists help solve are medico-legal, but a small percentage of cases deal with urban or stored-products entomology, and some even involve veterinary entomology, or the study of insects on animals other than humans. For example, when a hiker discovers a dead bear in the woods outside the usual hunting season, this is a case involving veterinary entomology. An urban entomology case might involve a termite infestation that contributed to a building collapse, while a stored-products case often begins with an unhappy telephone call to a food company from a consumer unfortunate enough to have eaten part of an insect-infested snack. Different criminal or civil issues may be involved, but forensic entomologists solve these cases in much the same way they would medico-legal cases.

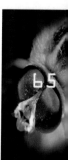

CHAPTER FOUR

Maggots Are Chocolate Lovers, Too

The woman was hungry. She stopped her vehicle outside a quaint roadside shop, imagining how delicious her favorite chocolate candies would taste. She bought a bag of the candies from the shop and began eating them as soon as she returned to her car. Only when she had eaten half of the candies in the bag did she really notice how terrible they tasted. Switching on the dome light to look into the bag, she saw a maggot on one of the candy pieces. Soon after this discovery, the woman called a lawyer and tried to sue the candy company for food contamination.

A team of forensic entomologists went to the roadside shop and purchased numerous snacks, including the chocolate candies about which the woman complained. Every item they opened contained maggots. The insect infestation was not the fault of the candy company but rather the fault of the store, which failed to rotate their food stock. When the woman's lawyers heard the scientific evidence they dropped their case against the candy company.

For the maggots, the chocolate candies were like fast food. The vulnerable maggots emerged from their eggs to find an

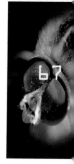

immediate food source, not to mention a safe living space inside the candy bag.

The food habits of some insects can be merely annoying or down right destructive. For example, ants and fruit flies invade the average home when there are crumbs or soft fruits to be eaten, but other insects such as termites (*Isoptera*) can destroy buildings and bridges with their taste for wood. Insects can infest human food long before it reaches the home.

Insects commonly invade stored foods, especially grain and rice, because food in storage gives insects a plentiful, convenient food source protected from predators, an ideal environment for growth, development, and reproduction. Granary weevils, flour moths, and grain moths typically infest stored grains

Termites feed on wood.

and rice. These insects can cause considerable destruction to food stores because not only do they eat the food but they also contaminate it with feces, shed exoskeletons (their tough, outer protective coverings), unwanted odors, and whole or parts of dead insects.

The preferences of some other insects may seem even more bizarre: the aptly named cigarette and drugstore beetles (family *Anobiidae*) eat tobacco and several commercial drugs.

Insects infest stored foods at any location between the food-processing plant and the consumer's home. The role of the

It's always best to watch what you eat—insects can infest and contaminate bushels of rice and grain.

CASE STUDY: BUGGY HEALTH FOOD

On a warm fall day in Florida, a health-conscious customer reached for a fruit and nut snack, only to see larvae through the transparent wrapper. The disgruntled customer telephoned the chief executive officer (CEO) of the snack company to complain, after which many other customers flooded the company with complaints and snack returns. The CEO hired a forensic entomologist to discover the origin and cause of the insect infestation. If the company's processing plant was not the source of the insect invasion, the company would need to report the forensic entomologist's findings to its insurance agency in order to receive compensation for damaged food stock.

The food company processed raw goods such as dried fruit, nuts, and grains into a health-food snack. Many different suppliers delivered these goods to the plant where workers processed and packed the final product in less than one week. The plant stored the snacks up to three months before shipping them to retail companies. When the forensic entomologist examined the infested product and the stored food at the factory, he identified the insect pest, larvae of the Indian meal moth. He also noticed the same moths stuck to sticky traps hanging in the facility and knew that the factory had had a series of moth outbreaks. Was the processing plant the source of the moth-infested grain?

Snacks sent to retail stores around the world at the same time as the infested product did not contain moth larvae. Since the packaging on these items was sealed, infestation at the retail stores was unlikely. The only possible alternative was that infested grain from one of numerous suppliers contaminated the grain supply at the factory. The forensic entomologist knew that humidity in dried foods is important for soft-bodied insect larvae to survive, and that humidity affects the rate at which Indian meal moth larvae develop into adults in a predictable way. In an environment with low humidity, the larvae would have developed slowly. He measured the humidity in the processing plant to calculate the rate at which the moth larvae would have developed into their present stages. Once he knew their development rate, he could determine when the moths first infested the food stores, which turned out to be the previous winter. Since the factory did not store food as long as a whole year, the forensic entomologist concluded the moths entered the factory in raw food materials from one of many suppliers. The food company later received an insurance claim settlement of over $250,000.

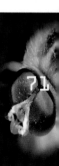

CASE STUDY: SWEPT UNDER THE RUG

A government official returning to his office was rankled when he noticed large maggots crawling along the threshold of his door. Although the cleaning woman assured him she cleaned the carpet every evening, and had in fact cleaned it the night before, he hesitated to believe her. The maggots were already one centimeter long, so they could not have grown that large in a single night. Thinking the maggots proved the cleaning woman had not cleaned the carpet in a long time, the government official fired her.

Later, a veterinarian inspecting the building examined the carpet in the official's office and collected some of the maggots, which he recognized as the blowfly species Lucilia sericata. According to him, the maggots were nearly ready to pupate. The maggots probably migrated from their food source, most likely a mouse or some forgotten food left over from a business lunch, to the carpet near the official's door. There, they would pupate and develop into adult flies. Realizing he was wrong, the government official asked the cleaning woman to return to work.

forensic entomologist is to determine the source of insect invasions in these food products.

The insect world contains a great diversity of species with different food preferences. While some insects have a seemingly bizarre taste for candy, grains, and even tobacco products, others prefer a diet of good old-fashioned carrion. In addition to infesting stored food products in homes and factories, insects may also create a comfortable dwelling between walls, under carpets, in attics and basements, and even inside the very wood that holds a building together, as long as an attractive food source is close by.

FOLLOW THOSE MAGGOTS!

Interestingly, some of the very same insects that feed on human remains also become cause for investigation when they infest homes, offices, and industrial warehouses. Flesh flies, which lay their eggs in the rotting meat of humans and other animals, are common household pests. If a home already has a rodent infestation and some of the rodents living in walls or attic spaces die, flesh flies may arrive to lay their eggs in the rotting flesh of these animals. Open dumpsters close to the outside of a building may also attract flesh flies and lead them to invade any cracks or openings in the nearby wall.

When maggots pass through the third instar of development, they move away from their food source and search for a safe, dry spot to pupate. Maggots will often migrate under rugs and furniture. To find the origin of an infestation, the forensic entomologist looks for a trail of maggots that leads back to their food source. The food source may even be a human body. A home infestation of insects important in medico-legal entomology may be the clue to a more serious case. Hiding a body in a closet, attic, or basement is not an uncommon practice for a criminal who does not wish to be caught. In this way, one case may involve both urban and medico-legal entomology.

Insects attracted to rotting flesh may be considered pests at times, but they can also be useful in a new application

important to wildlife biologists and conservationists. For example, some hunters prefer to avoid paying a fee that allows them to kill an animal, such as a deer, during the hunting season. A hunter who shoots a deer outside the hunting season is a poacher, or someone who kills an animal illegally. Capturing poachers is a difficult task for law enforcement, but forensic entomology may soon make the job a little easier.

PUTTING A STOP TO POACHING

Forensic entomologists have recently become involved in helping police track down poachers. One project in British Columbia aims to build a database that will help record how insects grow and develop on the carcasses of wild animals, the time of death of the animals, and whether they died outside of the usual hunting season. This information may lead to convicting more suspected poachers in the hopes of ending illegal hunting, a practice that has led to the decline of Canadian bear populations.

Late one summer, the RCMP called on a forensic entomologist to solve the case of two black bear cubs found dead near a dumpsite in Winnipeg, Manitoba. Someone had shot the cubs and taken their gallbladders, which fetch a high price at Asian markets due to their medicinal properties. The very same summer, poachers had also killed the cubs' mother and many other adult bears for the same reason.

Eyewitnesses reported hearing gunshots and seeing two men at the dumpsite where police found the cubs. A DNA test of blood from a bag belonging to the men matched blood taken from the cubs. However, the DNA evidence was not enough to convict the men of poaching. Police needed to know if the suspects had indeed been at the crime scene when the cubs died, so they turned to a forensic entomologist for help.

Police collected insect eggs from the carcasses and allowed them to develop for twenty-four hours. The forensic entomologist identified the insects hatched from the eggs as three species of blowfly. She could pinpoint the bears' time of death because she knew how long each blowfly species took to hatch, the temperature of the crime scene the night police suspected the bears to have died, and that the flies usually laid eggs in an animal's flesh one to two hours after the animal's death. By her calculation, the cubs died the same night eyewitnesses saw the two men at the dumpsite. The insect evidence soon helped send the two poachers to jail.

In the case of poaching, insect evidence helps conserve threatened wildlife populations. Similarly, the information forensic entomologists obtain from insects on human bodies helps protect human populations when catching a killer is at stake. Insects provide law enforcement with a tool that can help resolve a wide range of criminal and civil cases, from homicide to insect invasions of food supplies. However, insects are not the only evidence from the natural world that scientists can use to solve a mystery. Pollen grains, the tiny reproductive capsules of plants, are even smaller than insects—so small, in fact, that scientists can only see an individual pollen grain under a microscope—and yet these tiny particles have the power to prove or disprove a criminal's alibi.

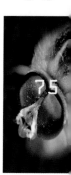

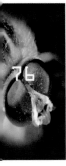

CHAPTER FIVE

Nature's Footprints

In an alleyway in a nondescript city, a woman was assaulted. But when she identified her alleged attacker, he denied the accusation. Hoping to convince authorities of his innocence, he stated that he had been in a nearby driveway at the time of the woman's assault. Unable to prove or disprove the suspect's alibi definitively, a law enforcement agent asked a local forensic palynologist for an expert evaluation of the evidence: pollen grains.

Just twenty-three feet (7 meters) separated the scene of the crime from the location of the alibi. The forensic palynologist collected soil samples from the alleyway where the crime took place, from the driveway where the suspect claimed to have been, and from the clothing the suspect wore at the time of the attack. Although the alleyway and the driveway were so close to each other, the two locations had significantly different types of plants. However, soil samples from the two sites had a similar number of different pollen types. Therefore the forensic palynologist was not surprised to find different *amounts* of these pollen types between the soil samples from each site. She next analyzed soil samples from the suspect's

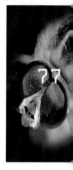

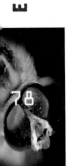

clothing. The amounts of different pollen types on the clothing correlated strongly with the amounts of different pollen types at the crime scene, but not with those from the driveway. "Nature's footprints," as some scientists call pollen, linked the suspect to the crime scene, destroying his alibi.

WHAT IS FORENSIC PALYNOLOGY?

Forensic palynology is the science of using *pollen* and *spores*—the reproductive capsules of plants and ferns, mosses, and fungi, respectively—to solve crimes and legal disputes. *Palynology*, the study of pollen and spores, forms the foundation of forensic palynology but generally involves making in-

Forensic palynologists study pollen and spores.

ferences about what landscapes looked like thousands and even millions of years ago. Both sciences involve similar questions: What plants grew in this location? Were there rivers, mountains, or oceans? The goal of forensic palynology is to use this information to reconstruct a sequence of human events that may help solve a crime.

Forensic palynologists, the scientists who examine pollen and spore evidence in legal cases, use this evidence for a variety of applications. Most often pollen and spores help link a suspect to an object or person in a crime scene or to the crime scene itself, as the above assault case showed. In the case of illicit drug trafficking, pollen can link several traffickers to the same drug supply and determine the source of the drugs. Pollen can also help pinpoint the origin of stolen merchandise or contaminated food. To avoid fraud and to create educational exhibits, museums may even use pollen analysis to evaluate the authenticity of any artwork they receive.

WHAT IS A FORENSIC PALYNOLOGIST?

A forensic palynologist examines pollen and spores in soil, dust, and mud; human or animal hair; packing materials, food, and illegal drugs; or from cars, buildings, and air filters to reconstruct recent human events, providing law enforcement agents, lawyers, and government agencies with valuable information. In contrast to the job of a forensic entomologist, a forensic palynologist mainly answers the question, *where* rather than *when*: Where was the suspect at the time of the crime? Where did the crime take place? Where did the illegal shipment of drugs, food products, or other goods come from?

The type of answer forensic palynologists and forensic entomologists have in common is *who*. When a forensic palynologist finds out where a crime took place, she may be able to match the types of pollen from the crime scene and a suspect's clothing to suggest he was at the scene of the crime or to support his alibi.

Similar to the job of a forensic entomologist, a forensic palynologist works in his laboratory and also testifies in a court of law. In a typical case, he may receive pollen and spore samples from soil at the crime scene, from the victim's clothing, skin, and hair, and from the clothing a suspect wore at the time law enforcement agents believe he committed the crime. The forensic palynologist carefully extracts pollen from the soil samples using different chemical processes that give him a final product of very concentrated pollen grains. From this sample, he identifies the plants to which the pollen belongs so that he can reconstruct the geographic area where the crime took place and where the suspect most likely was at the time

Better than a footprint: palynologists can trace evidence from samples taken from the bottom of a shoe.

of the crime. After long hours in the laboratory, he sends a report about his conclusions to the law enforcement agency.

If a case goes to trial, a forensic palynologist must testify. Testifying for a forensic palynologist is in some ways even more grueling than for a forensic entomologist because law enforcement agencies, scientists, and attorneys consider the evidence it provides less than reliable. Therefore, forensic palynology is less common than forensic entomology in most countries of the world except for New Zealand, which routinely allows palynological evidence in legal proceedings. In countries where forensic palynology is uncommon, forensic palynologists must be well prepared for detailed interrogation in the courtroom. Lawyers will attempt to cast doubt on a forensic palynologist's conclusions by trying to find a mistake in the way she or other scientists collected and transported the pollen samples from the crime scene to the laboratory, a process that can damage a sample, or in the way she extracted or identified the pollen. To prepare herself for the courtroom, a forensic palynologist always keeps a step-by-step record of her methods at the crime scene and in the laboratory.

THE EMERGING SCIENCE OF FORENSIC PALYNOLOGY

More recent than the application of insect evidence to criminal cases is the use of pollen and spores in these investigations. The first two cases in which forensic palynology played a significant role took place in Europe in 1959. In the early stages of forensic palynology, geologists and *criminalists*, in addition to palynologists, examined pollen and spore evidence. By the mid-twentieth century, palynologists analyzed pollen falling from plants onto soil and other surfaces to link suspects and victims to crime scenes.

By the 1960s and 1970s, scientists had already begun using pollen to link suspects with murder weapons and other objects from the crime scenes. A Swiss criminalist named Max Frei gained fame for his frequent use of pollen and spore evidence

CASE STUDIES: POLLEN CLUES

When an Austrian man disappeared on his trip down the Danube River, Wilhelm Klaus, a palynologist working at the University of Vienna, helped solve the mysterious disappearance using pollen evidence. He examined the muddy shoes of the man suspected of murdering the vacationer in 1959. In the caked mud he found spruce, willow, and alder pollen as well as hickory pollen. From this combination of pollen types he concluded that the victim's missing body might lie in a small area of the Danube Valley about twelve miles (20 kilometers) north of Vienna. When police informed the suspect of this information, the suspect confessed to the murder and led them to the buried body in the same area of the Danube Valley suggested in the pollen sample.

In the spring of 1959, Swedish police traced a victim's body back to the scene of the crime. An unknown attacker murdered a woman during her trip to central Sweden. Pollen from soil attached to her clothes suggested the suspect killed the woman and then moved the body to another location because the pollen did not belong to plants common in the area where authorities collected her body in May. The palynologist involved in the case expected to find pollen from certain herbs and grasses where the suspect left the body, but did not find them. However, if the murder occurred before May, these plants would not have released pollen, explaining the absence of their pollen on the victim's body.

in a variety of criminal cases during this time period. In one such case Frei used pollen and spore evidence to link a suspect with the murder weapon. The suspect claimed he had not removed his pistol from its box for months, and therefore he could not have shot the victim. However, pollen sticking to grease on the pistol came from alder and birch trees that would have released pollen at the time of the murder, not when the suspect claimed to have cleaned and packed away his pistol for the last time. Nature's silent witnesses—pollen grains—caught the killer in a lie.

Spores and pollen grains may stick to hair, skin, clothes, or even a murder weapon.

CASE STUDY: RULING OUT SUSPECTS
WITH POLLEN

Perhaps a major reason pollen evidence does not hold up in court is that pollen cannot prove without a doubt that a suspect was at a crime scene. However, it can certainly prove that a suspect was not at a crime scene. According to scientists M. Horrocks and K. A. J. Walsh in "Forensic Palynology: Assessing the Value of the Evidence," forensic palynologists find out where the victim or suspect was not.

If a forensic palynologist compares pollen from a suspect's shirt with pollen from the crime scene, the two samples must match perfectly to prove the suspect was at the crime scene. Ideally, the samples should have the same kinds and amounts of uncommon pollen, but two pollen samples are rarely identical, even if they come from the same soil. Like DNA, pollen more accurately serves as exculpatory evidence, that is, evidence that eliminates a suspect from the crime scene. The suspect's shirt is unlikely to be missing a unique pollen type found at the crime scene if she committed the crime. For example, if a crime occurred in a pine forest, the perpetrator will very likely have pine pollen on her clothes. If the suspect does indeed have pine pollen on her clothes or shoes, however, it does not prove she was at the crime scene because pine trees are very common and their pollen disperses over a large area. The suspect just as likely could have been walking her dog in the park or building a shed in her back yard as committing the crime. However, if the suspect did not have pine pollen on her clothes or shoes, she almost certainly was not in a pine forest and therefore probably did not commit the crime.

Although these tiny biological particles can help scientists, law enforcement officials, and government agencies gain valuable information, few countries use forensic palynology in criminal or civil cases. New Zealand leads the world in routinely using pollen and spores to solve crimes. In the United States and Canada, however, forensic palynology receives little recognition or credibility. Pollen and spores rarely provide information critical to solving a crime in North America for many reasons: not all law enforcement agencies are familiar with forensic palynology or its potential benefits; more familiar, traditional forensics methods such as DNA analysis already satisfy law enforcement agencies; evidence from pollen and spores usually does not withstand criticism in a court of law; few palynologists have the expert training needed for forensics work; few laboratories have the special equipment forensic palynologists need; and creating a laboratory with equipment to analyze pollen is extremely expensive.

Pollen evidence may not be widely accepted in North America, but this fact does not make forensic palynology any less remarkable. The wonder of forensic palynology is that the evidence that may incriminate or liberate a suspect is too small to be seen with the naked eye, and the many applications of forensic palynology would not be possible without the reproductive efforts of plants, ferns, mosses, and fungi.

CHAPTER SIX

Riding the Wind

Police uncover the body of a woman in a city park. The man suspected of attacking and murdering her denies ever having seen the victim or being in the wooded area where the body was found, but a wool sweater and dirt-caked pants he wore on the day of the crime suggest otherwise. When a forensic palynologist examines the suspect's clothing as well as a pair of shorts from the victim, she finds large amounts of pine pollen and fern spores. Soil samples from the wooded area where police found the woman's body also contain large amounts of pine pollen and fern spores, which place the suspect and the victim at the crime scene. The pollen and spores that stuck to the suspect's clothing as he struggled with the victim later help convict him of murder.

Pollen is all around us—in the food we eat and the air we breathe; in soil and buildings; in our hair and on our clothes; dusting vehicles parked on the street in springtime. Wind, water, and animals carry or disperse pollen to all of these places.

In general, neither the environment nor rigorous laboratory testing destroys a pollen sample. Individual pollen grains occur in a great diversity of shapes, sizes, and surface features specific to the plants from which they disperse and to the geographic region in which the plants grow. The fact that pollen is abundant, long-lasting, and unique to each type of plant makes it a valuable tool for solving crimes.

POLLEN DISPERSAL

Forensic palynology works because of the unique ways plants reproduce. Pollen contains the male reproductive cells of flowering and cone-producing plants such as corn (*Zea mays*),

Corn is a cone-producing plant.

clover (*Trifolium* species), and pine trees (*Pinus* species). The reproductive structures of ferns, mosses, and fungi are called spores. A strong outer wall protects the reproductive cells in pollen from harsh environments and soil microbes that might consider pollen a tasty meal. Characteristics of these outer walls are unique to each plant. Forensic palynologists use these characteristics to identify the plants to which different types of pollen belong.

Some plants release pollen that rides the wind in search of another plant to pollinate. Other plants produce sticky pollen that clings to the bodies of insects and the snouts of flower-feeding animals, eventually finding another flower to fertilize. Still other plants, such as ferns, reproduce by releasing spores from their fronds. The spores settle on the soil below and grow into mature plants.

Plants produce different amounts of pollen depending on the amount of light they receive, the climate in which they grow, and whether they must transport their pollen via wind, water, or animals.

The process of releasing pollen into the environment is called *dispersal*. Two types of dispersal patterns are particularly important to forensic palynologists: animal pollination and wind pollination.

Plants that rely on insects (bees, wasps, moths, and beetles) and other animals (hummingbirds, bats, and marsupials) for pollination are *zoogamous*. They are important to forensic palynology because their pollen grains possess some of the most durable outer walls that prevent decay and preserve pollen for long periods of time. These plants produce pollen in low amounts so that it is not a potential contaminant in a pollen sample. Pollen from these plants does not travel over large areas, so if pollen from one of these plants occurs in a pollen sample from a given area, more likely than not this pollen belongs in the area. However, these plants produce so little pollen that collecting a sample large enough to analyze often proves difficult.

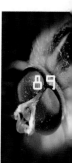

Anemophilus plants such as cone-bearing trees, some flowering plants, and a number of spore-producers such as fungi, ferns, and mosses, depend on wind for pollination. Wind pollination is the most inefficient pollination mode, requiring these plants and fungi to produce large amounts of lightweight pollen that travel easily to faraway places on the wind to increase the chance of pollinating others of their species. These plants provide more pollen for a forensic palynologist to analyze, increasing the likelihood of drawing an accurate conclusion from the evidence.

Pollen falling from plants or moving on the wind is called *pollen rain*. Forensic palynologists collect samples of this pollen rain from soil, hair, skin, clothing, food, and other surfaces. For instance, soil samples have unique *pollen spectra*, or types and amounts of pollen specific to the plants growing above the soil. The pollen spectrum in soil depends on the number and kinds of plants in the area and the times at which these plants release pollen. From a pollen spectrum a forensic palynologist can predict what kinds of plants grow in the area where he collected his soil sample.

This information particularly helps locate crime scenes and murder victims, and can prove or support alibis. If a suspect moved a victim's body in the hope of hiding the crime scene, the pollen spectrum of the soil on the victim or pollen rain falling on the victim's body can reveal where the crime actually occurred. Similarly, the types of pollen on a suspect's clothing can link him to the crime scene or to an object, such as a weapon or vehicle, from the crime scene.

The wind-pollinated corn plant (*Zea mays*) left a condemning fingerprint on a murder suspect in the North American Midwest. Police arrested a drifter for breaking into a closed liquor store. While in jail awaiting trial, the drifter complained to another inmate that he wouldn't be in jail if his car hadn't gotten stuck in the mud. The inmate reported this to the sheriff, who located the abandoned car thirty miles (48 kilometers) south of town. Near the car he found the body of a farmer, but

Due to the large amounts of pollen wind-pollinating plants produce, pollen rain may also contain pollen from locations besides the place where a forensic palynologist collected the sample. Plants of <u>Cannabis</u> species, or marijuana, produce up to 70,000 pollen grains per anther. Anthers are the stalk-like structures inside flowers that contain pollen and occur in different numbers according to the plant species. Traces of the plant's pollen on the shoes of someone suspected of possessing the drug could come from almost anywhere because the pollen disperses widely on the wind. For this reason, small amounts of the pollen found on a suspect or their belongings may not link them with a drug supply. An attempt to use trace amounts of the pollen as evidence of drug possession may not withstand examination in a court of law.

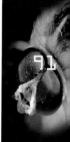

91

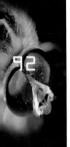

Some palynologists speculate lawyers for both the prosecution and the defense in the O. J. Simpson case lost a chance to present important evidence because they failed to consider pollen. Testimony suggested the suspect or suspects who attacked Simpson's wife and her friend hid in the bushes waiting for the victims prior to committing the crime. If Simpson hid in the bushes at the crime scene, as the prosecution argued, scientists could have looked for pollen or spores on the clothing he wore at the time of the crime. Pollen from the bushes on his clothing would have suggested he was at the crime scene and would have helped the prosecution. Alternatively, the absence of pollen or spores from the bushes on his clothing might have proven Simpson had not hidden in the bushes and may not have been at the crime scene at all, a valuable piece of evidence for the defense.

required more evidence to link the drifter to the man's murder. When the drifter refused to confess to the crime, police used pollen analysis to help determine whether he had been at the crime scene the day before. Pollen samples from the suspect's clothes revealed corn pollen in very high concentrations on the collar and shoulders of the suspect's shirt. A cornfield in full bloom separated the crime scene and the area in which the suspect abandoned the car from the highway along which eyewitnesses reportedly saw him walking the night of the murder. The density of pollen grains on the collar and shoulders of the shirt suggested the suspect ran through the cornfield because the blooming tassels would have been at shoulder height. As he ran, his neck and shoulders brushed against the corn plants, releasing large amounts of pollen. From the pollen analysis and additional evidence, police concluded the suspect murdered the farmer, stole and abandoned his car, and then ran through the cornfield to the highway leading to town, hoping to escape the law.

In the case of a fatal plane crash, pollen evidence helped a jury decide in favor of, rather than against, the defendants. The plaintiffs claimed a mass of plant materials clogging a small part of the fuel line caused the plane to crash, and that the plant matter accumulated suddenly or gradually over the lifetime of the engine. To find out whether the plaintiffs' statement was correct, investigators needed to determine when and how the plant mass accumulated in the fuel line. Forensic palynologists analyzed a clump of pollen attached to the plant mass.

First, forensic palynologists identified the types of pollen in the plant mass. They found mostly gumweed (family *Compositae*) and sweet clover (family *Leguminosae*). Both of these plants grew in the area around the storage yard where the plaintiffs kept the plane wreckage. Most interestingly, both plants are insect-pollinated, and only 1.1 percent of the pollen from the fuel line came from wind-pollinated plants. The pollen from the gumweed and sweet clover plants could not

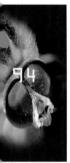

have entered the fuel line while the plane was in flight because pollen from insect-pollinated plants does not disperse widely on the wind.

When the plane crashed, it burned for many hours at temperatures high enough to distort the body of the plane. Forensic palynologists charred pollen grains from gumweed and sweet clover plants in the storage yard at 400 degrees Fahrenheit (250 degrees Celsius) for five minutes and compared these pollen grains to the ones they collected from the fuel line. When they looked at the pollen under an SEM, the forensic palynologists saw the charred pollen was nearly destroyed. The pollen from the fuel line, however, was not damaged at all. In fact, the pollen from the plane was so healthy that forensic

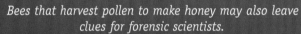

Bees that harvest pollen to make honey may also leave clues for forensic scientists.

palynologists were able to make the grains start growing in the laboratory. Had the pollen been in the fuel line at the time of the crash, it would have been too damaged to *germinate*.

Last of all, forensic palynologists used the color of pollen grains to determine whether the pollen from the plane entered the fuel line before or after the crash. Had the pollen been exposed to extreme heat, it would have been dark in color. Instead, the pollen in the fuel line was bright yellow, typical of fresh pollen.

Forensic palynologists concluded that plant mass clogging the fuel line must have accumulated after the crash while the plane wreckage was in storage. But how did the plant mass get there?

Investigators suspected nest-building bees (family *Megachilidae*) were the culprits, because plant matter clogged the fuel line on only one side of the plane. These bees build nests in tunnels and openings with materials from the natural environment. When they inspected the wreckage, investigators found nest-building bees in parts stored with the remnants of the plane, as well as a hair from one of the bees in the mass of plant matter. The plant mass was indeed a bees' nest. From this evidence the jury ruled out the plaintiffs' explanation for the crash, deciding in favor of the defendants.

STICKING TO IT: POLLEN EVIDENCE ON STOLEN OR IMPORTED GOODS

Of any material upon which pollen and spores fall, hair is the best trap. Pollen and spores traveling on the wind stick between individual strands of hair belonging to a victim, suspect, domestic or farm animal, or any material object containing hair or fur such as rugs, vehicle seat covers, and clothing. Hair or other fibers with added oil or other sticky products such as hairspray trap pollen and spores even more effectively.

A rustler once learned this difficult lesson when pollen grains revealed he had stolen three hundred sheep. Weeks after

stealing the sheep from another farmer's ranch and leaving not a trace of evidence behind, the rustler attempted to sell a herd of 350 sheep at a local auction. However, the auctioneer knew this farmer owned hardly enough land to raise 200, let alone 350 of them. Police impounded the sheep. The farmer who had reported his sheep missing weeks ago arrived, looked at the sheep, and told police they more than likely belonged to him. Since he had no receipt and the sheep lacked brands, the farmer could not prove his ownership. The rustler claimed he bought the sheep, but he refused to tell police where he purchased them and could not show a receipt of the sale.

Police turned to pollen analysis to determine the animals' owner. They carefully sheared small samples of wool from the

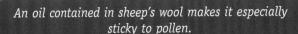

An oil contained in sheep's wool makes it especially sticky to pollen.

sheep's backs and sent the wool to a laboratory for analysis. Sheep's wool contains lanolin, oil that protects the wool from moisture and helps keep sheep warm in wet weather. Pollen sticks especially well to oily or sticky surfaces, so a forensic palynologist would expect to find a promising amount of pollen to analyze in a sample of sheep's wool. The results in this case forced the rustler to hand over most of the sheep when pollen from three hundred of them matched the types of plants growing in the field from which he stole them and not those in his own pasture.

Customs agents use pollen analysis to decide whether to allow certain imported goods into the United States or Canada. To make this kind of decision, customs agents must know the origin of the goods. On one occasion when a shipment of Persian rugs arrived in the United States, customs agents inspecting the rugs suspected they came from Iran. The rug owners insisted they came from Egypt, however. Pollen analysis would determine whether customs agents permitted the rugs to enter the country, since at that time, the United States did not allow trade with Iran. Samples of dust and soil collected from the rugs with a vacuum cleaner contained pollen types matching those a palynologist would expect to find in both Iran *and* Egypt. Some types of pollen in the samples matched plants more common in Iran than Egypt, but since the palynologist did not have any samples from these countries with which to make a comparison, pollen analysis could not prove the rugs' origin. Due to these inconclusive results, customs agents allowed the owners to import their rugs.

AUTHENTICITY: ART AND HONEY

Museums often wish to determine the authenticity of the art they own, ranging from textiles to sculptures or paintings, especially if they receive these works as a gift.

Several years ago, for example, the Royal Ontario Museum in Toronto received the Gondar Hanging, a large cord-woven silk hanging of religious and artistic significance. Ethiopian

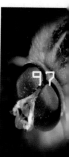

In 2002, 8,884 bee-keepers exported 21,914 tons of honey worth 87.9 million U.S. dollars according to Canada's AgriFood Trade Service.

artisans most likely created the Gondar Hanging in the late seventeenth or early eighteenth century. In 1993–1994, art conservationists at the Canadian Conservation Institute cleaned and restored the hanging. Curators from the Royal Ontario Museum asked the art conservationists to verify the authenticity of the artwork as well. If the hanging did indeed come from Ethiopia, pollen samples taken from between its fibers and from the packing material in which it arrived at the museum would match pollen from plants growing in Ethiopia at the time of the hanging's creation. The results of pollen analysis revealed water willow (*Justica* species) and olive (*Olea chrysophylla*) plants common in Ethiopia, the Mediterranean, and North Africa. Since neither plant grows in Canada, the Royal Ontario Museum knew the hanging most likely came from Ethiopia or North Africa.

Authenticity is also important to consumers. When people choose which food brand to buy, they often base their decision on the geographic origin of the product. Honey is an excellent example. Since many customers may choose what kind of honey to buy according to the location of the *apiary*, and the types of plants from which the bees made the honey, apiaries label their honey with this information in hope of selling more of their product. For example, Canada is the world's sixth-largest producer of honey, exporting honey to twenty-five countries including the United States.

Canadian honey is considered to be of fine quality among connoisseurs.

CASE STUDY: DISHONEST BEEKEEPERS

Pollen analysis helped the USDA determine whether a large shipment of domestic honey it purchased as part of a farm subsidy program came from apiaries in the United States only. To receive a government subsidy, beekeepers had to pledge their honey was purely domestic. At the time of the subsidy program, the price of foreign honey was much lower than honey produced in the United States. Therefore, beekeepers could make a quick but illegal profit from buying cheap imported honey and selling it to the USDA under the subsidy program, falsely labeling the honey "domestically produced." The Office of the United States Inspector General, which supervised the subsidy program, suspected some of the USDA-purchased honey was imported. Analysis of pollen in honey samples over a three-year period showed between 6 and 10 percent of the honey came from Latin America.

Honey enthusiasts enjoy Canadian honey for its mild taste and clear appearance, attributable to the plants growing in the country's prairies: clover, alfalfa, and canola. To market their honey to international customers as well as Canadian consumers, who may prefer to buy a local product over an imported one, Canadian apiaries advertise this information on honey jars. Apiaries may test the authenticity of their own honey before they add geographic and botanical information to their labels. The Canadian Food Inspection Agency monitors honey safety and quality. The strict regulations of the

Strict regulation of honey production protects the consumer.

Canadian Agricultural Products Act require beekeepers to include the plant source of their honey on package labels. Such honesty protects beekeepers who sell authentic honey and helps consumers make informed buying decisions.

Some apiaries might falsely label their honey. For example, a jar labeled "100% clover honey, made in the U.S.A." could contain honey from various other plants growing outside the country. In the United States, the United States Food and Drug Administration (FDA) regulates the quality and safety of commercial honey, and the United States Department of Agriculture (USDA) regulates the importation and exportation of honey. If the USDA suspects an apiary of fraudulent labeling, for example, palynologists extract pollen samples from the honey to determine the geographic origin of the product, the types of plants the bees used to make the honey (its *botanical origin*), and the purity of the honey. Bees use plant nectar to make honey, which often contains pollen grains from the plants the bees visited. Palynologists record the different types of pollen in the honey to discover which plants the bees visited. Pollen from plants growing in specific geographic locations can reveal the region from which the honey came.

DRUG-TRAFFICKING

Pollen residue on illegal drugs and on the clothes of persons suspected of manufacturing, distributing, or abusing these drugs can help law enforcement agents reconstruct the route by which a shipment of illegal drugs entered the United States or Canada and can link suspects with a confiscated drug sample. Forensic palynologists collect this information by comparing pollen samples from the drugs, the suspect's clothing, and the location from which the drugs are suspected to have originated.

For example, the manufacturing process of cocaine involves many stages in which different types of pollen may enter the drug supply. As workers harvest, dry, and process coca leaves in the open air before processing them into cocaine, pollen from the coca plants and other nearby plants often settles on the final product. If a forensic palynologist finds in a drug sample pollen grains from plants that only grow in particular regions of the world, countries, or even states, they may be able to provide law enforcement officials with information about the source of the drugs, where different stages of the manufacturing process occurred, and the probability that the suspects in question are guilty of drug possession or drug trafficking.

In one such case in the early 1990s, New York City police seized a 500-gram shipment of cocaine and worked with Dr.

Trace evidence found on confiscated drugs may leave clues to its origin.

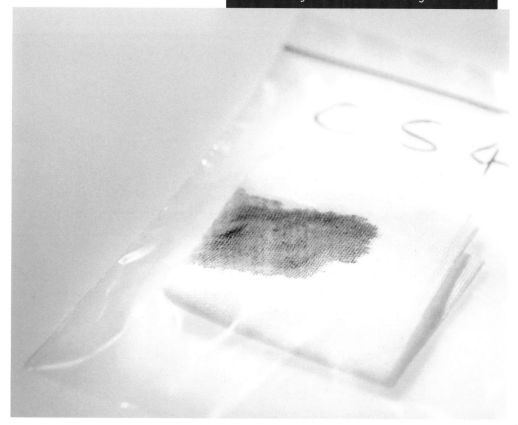

Edward Stanley, a forensic palynologist, to reconstruct the route by which the shipment arrived in New York City. Pollen analysis revealed three distinct types of pollen. The first pollen types came from tropical plants known to grow in Bolivia and Columbia and most likely mixed with the drug sample when workers picked and processed the coca leaves into coca paste. Jack pine (*Pinus banksiana*) and Canadian hemlock (*Tsuga canadensis*) made up the second group of pollen types. These trees grow in the cool northern regions of the United States, such as northern Michigan or Wisconsin, mountain areas along the Canadian border of northern New York, and the northern mountains of Maine and New Hampshire. These pollen types most likely settled on the drug sample when drug traffickers

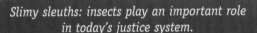

Slimy sleuths: insects play an important role in today's justice system.

added other substances to the cocaine and then packaged it before selling it. The forensic palynologist matched the last group of pollen types in the drug sample to weed plants growing in the vacant lots of downtown New York City and Manhattan Island. From this analysis, the New York City police could be fairly certain that the cocaine originated in South America where workers processed it for the first time. Smugglers then transported the drugs to the northeastern United States where they added other materials to the drugs and processed them, sending them on to New York City. Drug traffickers in New York City again mixed other substances into the cocaine and had just prepared the drugs for distribution when New York police seized the illegal shipment.

EVIDENCE FROM NATURE

The natural world pulses and buzzes with life at many scales. Glancing at a leaf reveals a caterpillar enjoying a juicy, green lunch; a closer look at the same leaf reveals tiny yellow pollen grains that drifted to earth on the wind. Small creatures play a large role in criminal justice, and perhaps what is most wondrous about them is that they are all around us, silently and swiftly leaving their marks, while even the most cunning of criminals are unaware.

The appetite of hungry young flies puts murderers behind bars while a plant's search for a mate incriminates a drug trafficker walking through a meadow. All too often, insects and pollen grains become the voices for those who can no longer speak for themselves. The dedication and expertise of forensic scientists continues to bring criminals to justice with the help of evidence from nature.

Glossary

apiary: A place where beehives are kept and bees are raised for honey.

civil: Involving individuals or groups in legal action other than criminal proceedings.

controlled experiment: An experiment involving a comparison between a group exposed to certain variables and a group not exposed to these variables to determine whether these variables caused the observed results.

criminalists: People who apply scientific techniques to the collection and analysis of physical evidence in criminal cases.

customs agents: Government employees who are responsible for collecting taxes on imports and for the prevention of illegal imports.

germinate: To start to grow from a seed or spore into a new individual.

habitat: The natural conditions and environment in which a plant or animal lives.

macabre: Including gruesome and horrific details of death and decay.

maggots: Worm-shaped larvae of the fly family found in decaying matter.

medical examiner: A physician appointed by the state or local government to establish the cause of someone's death.

medieval: Belonging to or typical of the European Middle Ages.

metabolic: Typical of metabolism, the series of chemical interactions taking place in organisms that provide the energy and nutrients needed to sustain life.

metamorphosis: The development of a larval insect into an adult.

postmortem interval (PMI): The period between the victim's death and the discovery of the body.

predatory: Characteristic of animals that survive by preying on others.

temperate: A range of temperatures within moderate limits.

velocity injury: An injury caused by speed.

Further Reading

Byrd, J. H., and J. L. Castner. *Forensic Entomology: The Utility of Arthropods in Legal Investigations*. Boca Raton, Fla.: CRC Press, 2000.

Crompton, C. W. *Pollen Grains of Canadian Honey Plants*. Gatineau, Quebec: Canadian Museum of Civilization, 1993.

Eisner, T. *For Love of Insects*. Cambridge, Mass.: Harvard University Press, 2003.

Evans, C. *Casebook of Forensic Detection: How Science Solved 100 of the World's Most Baffling Crimes*. Hoboken, N.J.: John Wiley and Sons, Inc., 1998.

Genge, N. *Forensic Casebook: The Science of Crime Scene Investigation*. New York: Ballantine Books, 2002.

Goff, M. Lee. *A Fly for the Prosecution: How Insect Evidence Helps Solve Crimes*. Cambridge, Mass.: Harvard University Press, 2000.

Gullan, P. J., and P. S. Cranston. *The Insects: An Outline of Entomology*. Williston, Vt.: Blackwell Science Inc., 2000.

Hoyt, E. *Insect Lives: Stories of Mystery and Romance from a Hidden World*. Cambridge, Mass.: Harvard University Press, 2002.

McKnight, B. E. *The Washing Away of Wrongs: Forensic Medicine in Thirteenth-century China*. Ann Arbor: University of Michigan Press, 1981.

Nilsson, S., and J. Praglowski, eds. *Erdtman's Handbook of Palynology*. Copenhagen: Munksgaard, 1992.

Peterson, R. T., ed. *Peterson First Guide to Insects of North America*. Boston, Mass.: Houghton Mifflin, 1998.

Pollan, M. *Botany of Desire: A Plants-Eye View of the World*. New York: Random House Inc., 2002.

Ramsland, K. M. *Forensic Science of C.S.I.* New York: Berkley Publishing Group, 2001.

Raven, P. H., S. E. Eichhorn, and R. F. Every. *Biology of Plants.* New York: W. H. Freeman & Co., 1998.

Sachs, J. S. *Corpse: Nature, Forensics and the Struggle to Pinpoint Time of Death.* New York: Perseus Books Group, 2002.

For More Information

The American Board of Forensic Entomology
web.missouri.edu/%7Eagwww/entomology

The Canadian Society of Forensic Science
www.csfs.ca

Career Information
www.sfu.ca/~ganderso

Climate Data from the National Oceanic and Atmospheric Administration
www.noaa.gov

Cornell University Pollen Image Database
www.cimc.cornell.edu/biog401/bio_images2.htm

Current Research at Texas A&M University
insects.tamu.edu

Insect Biology
www.earthlife.com/insects

Scanning Electron Microscope
www.mos.org/sln/SEM/index.html

The United States Department of Agriculture
www.usda.gov

The United States Federal Bureau of Investigation
www.fbi.gov

Publisher's note:
The Web sites listed on this page were active at the time of publication. The publisher is not responsible for Web sites that have changed their addresses or discontinued operation since the date of publication. The publisher will review and update the Web-site list upon each reprint.

Index

Picture Credits

Benjamin Stewart: pp. 26, 37
Comstock: p. 58
Corbis: p. 15
Corel p. 55
Eclecticollections: pp. 27, 28
Evangeline Ehl: pp. 40, 62, 64
Photos.com: pp. 10, 13, 18, 29, 30, 32, 39, 46, 49, 50, 51, 53, 63, 68, 69, 78, 80, 83, 88, 94, 96, 99, 101, 104
Stockbyte: pp. 56, 103

To the best knowledge of the publisher, all other images are in the public domain. If any image has been inadvertently uncredited, please notify Harding House Publishing Service, Vestal, New York 13850, so that rectification can be made for future printings.

Biographies

AUTHOR

Maryalice Walker grew up in Falmouth, Maine, and is an alumna of Smith College in Northampton, Massachusetts. She currently studies bat ecomorphology at the University of Cape Town, South Africa. Her research interests include the ecology and reproductive biology of flying animals. In her spare time, she enjoys writing, hiking, and spending time with her family.

SERIES CONSULTANTS

Carla Miller Noziglia is Senior Forensic Advisor, Tanzania, East Africa, for the U.S. Department of Justice, International Criminal Investigative Training Assistant Program. A Fellow of the American Academy of Forensic Sciences, Ms. Noziglia is Chair of the Board of Trustees of the Forensic Science Foundation since 2001. Her work has earned her many honors and commendations, including Distinguished Fellow from the American Academy of Forensic Sciences (2003) and the Paul L. Kirk Award from the American Academy of Forensic Sciences Criminalistics Section. Ms. Noziglia's publications include *The Real Crime Lab* (coeditor, 2005), *So You Want to be a Forensic Scientist* (coeditor 2003), and contributions to *Drug Facilitated Sexual Assault* (2001), *Convicted by Juries, Exonerated by Science: Case Studies in the Use of DNA* (1996), and the *Journal of Police Science* (1989). She is on the editorial board of the *Journal for Forensic Identification*.

Jay A. Siegel is Director of the Forensic and Investigative Sciences Program in the School of Science at Indiana University, Purdue University, Indianapolis. Dr. Siegel is a Fellow of the American Academy of Forensic Sciences, and is a member of the Forensic Science Society (England) and the editorial board of the *Journal of Forensic Sciences*. His publications include chapters in *Analytical Methods in Forensic Science* (1991), *Forensic Science* (2002), and *Forensic Science Handbook, vol. 2*. He is the coauthor of the upcoming college textbook *Fundamentals of Forensic Science*. Dr. Siegel has also appeared as an expert witness in many trials and as a forensic expert on television news programs.